English

The 11+
Study Book
and Parents' Guide

Practise • Prepare • Pass
Everything your child needs for 11+ success

CONTENTS

Section Four — Word Types

Section Five — Comprehension

Section Six — Writing

Published by CGP

Editors:
Luke Antieul, Claire Boulter, Heather Gregson, Anthony Muller, Holly Poynton, Jo Sharrock

Contributors:
Paul Warnes

With thanks to Glenn Rogers, Jennifer Underwood and Janet Berkeley for the proofreading.

With thanks to Jan Greenway for the copyright research.

ISBN: 978 1 84762 838 1
Website: www.cgpbooks.co.uk
Printed by Elanders Ltd, Newcastle upon Tyne.
Clipart from CorelDRAW®

Based on the classic CGP style created by Richard Parsons.

Photocopying – it's dull, grey and sometimes a bit naughty. Luckily, it's dead cheap, easy and quick
to order more copies of this book from CGP – just call us on 0870 750 1242. Phew!

What's in the 11+

Make sure you've got your head around the basics of the 11+ before you begin.

The 11+ is an Admissions Test

1) The 11+ is a test used by <u>some schools</u> to help with their <u>selection process</u>.

2) You'll usually take it when you're in <u>Year 6</u>, at some point during the <u>autumn term</u> or early in the <u>spring term</u>.

3) The schools <u>use the results</u> to decide who to accept. They might also use <u>other things</u> to help make up their minds, such as a short <u>interview</u> or information about <u>where you live</u>.

Some Schools test a Mixture of Subjects

1) Depending on the <u>school</u>, the 11+ might test <u>different subjects</u>.

2) There are <u>four</u> main subjects that can be tested in the 11+, so you might sit papers on <u>some</u> or <u>all</u> of these:

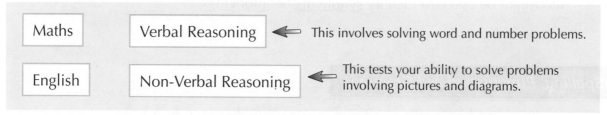

| Maths | Verbal Reasoning | ← This involves solving word and number problems. |
| English | Non-Verbal Reasoning | ← This tests your ability to solve problems involving pictures and diagrams. |

3) This book will help you with the <u>English</u> part of the test.

Get to Know what Kind of Paper you're taking

Your paper will either be <u>Multiple Choice</u> or <u>Standard Answer</u>.

Multiple Choice

1) For each question you'll be given some <u>options</u> on a <u>separate answer sheet</u>.

2) You'll need to mark your answer with a clear pencil <u>line</u> in the box next to the <u>option</u> that you think is <u>correct</u>.

Standard Answer

1) There won't be any <u>options</u> to choose from for <u>most questions</u>.

2) You'll usually <u>write</u> your answer on the <u>question paper</u>.

Look out for the 'Tips and Tricks' boxes in this Study Book — they'll give you practical advice about the test.

Make sure you check which type of <u>question paper</u> you'll be taking, so you know what it <u>looks</u> like and <u>where</u> your answers go. Try to do some practice tests in the <u>format</u> of the test you'll be taking, so you know what to <u>expect</u> on the day.

What's in the 11+ English Test

Get your brain ready for 11+ English by reading about the different question types.

11+ English will test your Reading and Word Knowledge

1) You'll already have <u>picked up</u> loads of the <u>skills</u> you need for the test <u>at school</u>.

2) There are three <u>main types</u> of <u>questions</u> that can crop up:

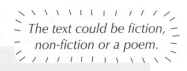

The text could be fiction, non-fiction or a poem.

Comprehension

You'll be given one <u>long</u> text or several <u>short</u> texts to read. You'll have to answer <u>questions</u> which test how well you <u>understand</u> the text. The questions might ask you about:

- what the text <u>means</u> — what <u>happens</u> in the text, what a <u>character</u> is like or how they <u>feel</u>, or what the writer's <u>purpose</u> is.
- <u>word meanings</u> — what some of the trickier words in the text <u>mean</u>.
- <u>word types</u> — whether a word is a <u>noun</u>, <u>verb</u> or another <u>part of speech</u>. You might be asked to identify <u>synonyms</u> or <u>antonyms</u>.

Spelling, Punctuation and Grammar

- You'll have to find <u>spelling</u> and <u>punctuation mistakes</u> in a short text, or <u>add punctuation marks</u> to sentences.
- For <u>grammar</u> questions, you'll usually need to <u>choose</u> the <u>best word</u> from a list of <u>options</u> to fill gaps in a text so that it makes sense.

Writing

Some tests include a <u>writing</u> task. You'll get a <u>title</u> or <u>topic</u> and you'll have between 20 minutes and an hour to write a <u>short story</u> or <u>essay</u>. You might have to continue the extract used in the <u>comprehension part</u> of the test. You'll need to:

- write in <u>standard English</u> (that means <u>no slang</u> or <u>text speak</u>).
- make sure your writing is <u>structured</u> with a beginning, a middle and an end.
- use plenty of <u>techniques</u> to make your writing <u>interesting</u>.

3) Some tests include <u>shorter tasks</u> that test your <u>word knowledge</u>. You might have to find the <u>odd one out</u> from a list of words, make <u>compound words</u>, <u>reorder words</u> to make a sentence, or <u>reorder sentences</u> to make a story.

4) You need to have a good <u>vocabulary</u> and to understand how words and sentences are <u>made</u>.

How to Prepare for the 11+

Give yourself a head start with your preparation — be organised and plan ahead.

Divide your Preparation into Stages

1) Find a way to prepare for the 11+ that <u>suits you</u>. This may depend on <u>how much time</u> you have before the test. Here's a good way to <u>plan</u> your English practice:

> Do the Benchmark Test at the front of this book. Ask an adult to mark it for you.
>
> ⬇
>
> Learn strategies for answering different question types using this Study Book.
>
> ⬇
>
> Do plenty of practice questions, concentrating on the question types you find tricky.
>
> ⬇
>
> Sit some practice papers to prepare you for the real test.

2) When you <u>first</u> start answering English questions, try to answer the questions without <u>making any mistakes</u>, rather than working <u>quickly</u>.

3) Once you feel <u>confident</u> about the questions, then you can build up your <u>speed</u>.

4) You can do this by asking an adult to <u>time</u> you as you answer a <u>set of questions</u>, or by seeing <u>how many</u> questions you can answer in a certain <u>amount of time</u>, e.g. 5 minutes. You can then try to <u>beat</u> your time or score.

5) As you get closer to the test day, work on getting a <u>balance</u> between <u>speed</u> and <u>accuracy</u> — that's what you're <u>aiming for</u> when you sit the real test.

There are Many Ways to Practise the Skills you Need

The <u>best way</u> to tackle 11+ English is to do lots of <u>practice</u>. This isn't the only thing that will help though — there are other things you can do to <u>build up the skills</u> you need for the test:

1) Read a lot, and make sure you read a mix of <u>fiction</u> and <u>non-fiction</u> writing.

2) If you're reading an <u>article</u> in a newspaper or magazine, <u>underline</u> the <u>key facts</u> as you read — picking out the most <u>important information</u> from a text is a really <u>useful skill</u>.

3) If you come across any <u>unfamiliar words</u>, look them up in a <u>dictionary</u>. Keep a <u>vocabulary list</u> to make sure you <u>remember</u> new words.

4) Play <u>word games</u> or do <u>crosswords</u> to build up your <u>vocabulary</u>.

5) <u>Write stories</u>, <u>letters</u> to friends and relatives or <u>articles</u> to go with news headlines that you find <u>interesting</u>. You could also <u>keep a diary</u> to practise your writing skills.

Sentences and Clauses

Your sentences will be crystal clear if you learn how to use phrases and clauses properly.

Warm-Up Activity

Write down <u>as many different sentences</u> as you can using only the options below.

make sure you wear your top hat   play your violin   to   eat frogs' legs

but   and
        let's go birdwatching   so   you have to be up early tomorrow

A **Sentence Always** has a **Verb**

Verbs can also be 'being' words, e.g. in the sentence 'I am cold', the verb is 'am'.

1) Verbs are <u>action</u> words — they describe what the <u>subject</u> of the sentence is <u>doing</u>.

'Andy' is the subject because he is 'doing' the action. | Andy baked a cake. | 'baked' is the verb.

Running is good for your health. | 'Running' is the subject because the verb 'is' describes what the subject does.

2) The subject and verb <u>have to agree</u>. This just means that a <u>singular subject</u> needs a <u>singular form</u> of the verb, and a <u>plural subject</u> needs a <u>plural form</u> of the verb.

Majid is in the car.   Majid and Neha are in the car.

The verb is 'is'. It's also singular.

The subject is 'Majid'. This is singular, as there is only one person.

The subject here is 'Majid and Neha' — there's more than one person, so this is plural.

The verb 'are' is also plural, to match the subject.

Phrases and **Clauses** Add Information to a **Sentence**

<u>Phrases</u> and <u>clauses</u> are groups of words that are used to form sentences.

A **Phrase Doesn't** have a **Verb**...

A phrase <u>doesn't</u> contain a verb, so it doesn't make sense <u>on its own</u>.

Jade wore her new purple dress.   Duncan put his hands in his pockets.

'her new purple dress' is a phrase.   'in his pockets' is a phrase.

...But a **Clause Does**

A clause is the same as a phrase — except that it <u>contains</u> a verb.

Suzy listened to the radio while she brushed her teeth.

This is a clause. The verb is 'brushed'.

Compound Sentences are made from Two Equal Clauses

1) A compound sentence is made of two clauses joined by a connective like 'or', 'and' or 'but'.
2) Each clause would make sense as a sentence on its own.

Martin sat down on the beach.   He fell asleep on the sand.

Stick the two clauses together using a
connective to make a compound sentence.

A connective is a 'joining' word. There's more on p.14.

Martin sat down on the beach and he fell asleep on the sand.

Complex Sentences have Main and Dependent Clauses

1) A complex sentence is made up of an important clause and one or more less important clauses.
2) The important clause is called the main clause. It makes sense on its own.
3) The other clauses are called dependent clauses — they don't make sense without the main clause.

I cleaned the house while you were out.

This is the main clause — it
makes sense on its own.

This is the dependent clause — you need to read
the main clause to understand what's happening.

Dependent clauses are also called subordinate clauses.

4) The dependent clause can be at the beginning, middle or end of the sentence.
5) Dependent clauses start with connectives. If the dependent clause is at the beginning of the sentence, it is separated from the main clause with a comma.

Learn to spot Phrases, Main Clauses and Dependent Clauses

Q Identify whether these are phrases, main clauses or dependent clauses.
   a) *bright blue eyes*   d) *last Saturday night*
   b) *Jane is late for work*   e) *after I finish my lunch*
   c) *if you see a dolphin*   f) *let's go shopping*

Method — Start by picking out the phrases

1) Start by finding the examples that don't have verbs. These are the phrases.

   a) bright blue eyes   d) last Saturday night   a) and d) are both phrases —
                                                       they add information to a sentence.

2) Then look for dependent clauses — these won't make sense on their own.

   c) if you see a dolphin   e) after I finish my lunch   c) and e) are dependent clauses because they
                                                            contain verbs but don't make sense on their own.

3) Finally look for main clauses — these can form sentences on their own.

   b) Jane is late for work   f) let's go shopping   b) and f) are main clauses — they contain
                                                        verbs and make sense on their own.

Section One — Grammar

Make sure that you can Recognise Sentence Types

Q Read this passage and then answer the questions that follow.

Polar bears live in the Arctic. They are the largest land carnivores in the world and an adult male can weigh up to 700 kg. Polar bears typically hunt seals but they will also eat reindeer, walruses, birds, eggs and shellfish. The number of polar bears has declined in recent years due to hunting and loss of sea ice.

a) *Write down a complex sentence from the passage.*
b) *Write down a compound sentence from the passage.*
c) *Write down a dependent clause from the passage.*

Method — Identify each sentence in the passage

Go through the passage and identify each sentence as you go along.

Polar bears live in the Arctic. ← This sentence is made up of a <u>main clause</u>. It isn't needed for the questions.

They are the largest land carnivores in the world and an adult male can weigh up to 700 kg.

This sentence is a compound sentence — it has two <u>main clauses</u> and a connective ('and'). This is one answer to b).

Polar bears typically hunt for seals but they will also eat reindeer, walruses, birds, eggs and shellfish.

This is another compound sentence. It could also be the answer to part b).

The number of polar bears has declined in recent years due to hunting and loss of sea ice.

This sentence is a complex sentence. The first part is a <u>main clause</u> and the second part is a <u>dependent clause</u>. It's the answer to part a).

The <u>second clause</u> is the answer to part c).

Practice Questions

1) Underline the main clause in each sentence below.
   a) *Before I go to bed, I always <u>brush my teeth</u>.*
   b) *In three months' time, <u>the gardener is retiring</u>.*
   c) *<u>Bruce can't go swimming</u> because he's got an upset stomach.*
   d) *<u>We'll eat now</u>, and then go for a run.*

2) Write down whether these sentences are compound sentences or complex sentences.
   a) *After scoring a goal, the footballer ran away to celebrate.* Complex
   b) *The weather was sunny and there were no clouds in the sky.* Compound
   c) *There's only twenty minutes until he will be here.* Complex
   d) *We could play rounders or we could go swimming.* Compound

Nouns and Pronouns

Learning about nouns and pronouns should be a walk in the park — you use them all the time.

Warm-Up Activity

These words are called collective nouns (see below).

Match each word in blue with the group it belongs to.

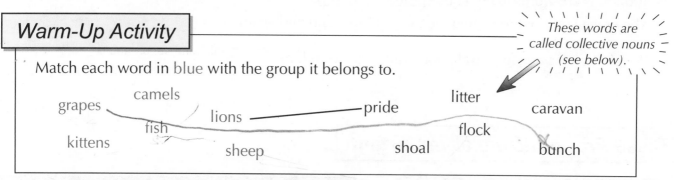

grapes   camels   lions ——— pride   litter   caravan
kittens   fish   sheep   shoal   flock   bunch

A **Noun** is the **Name Given** to **Something**

There are three types of noun that you need to know about:

1) *Proper Nouns are Names*

1) Proper nouns are the names of particular <u>people</u>, <u>places</u> or <u>things</u>.
2) They <u>always</u> start with a <u>capital letter</u>.

Your name is a proper noun.

> Heather is going to Rome.

'Heather' and 'Rome' are proper nouns.

> Let's go to Froggatt's Foods on Thursday.

'Froggatt's Foods' and 'Thursday' are also proper nouns.

2) *Common Nouns are Things*

1) Common nouns are names for people or things <u>in general</u>.
They <u>don't</u> usually start with a <u>capital letter</u>.

> Eat your banana at the table.

'banana' and 'table' are common nouns.

> That man is carrying a suitcase.

'man' and 'suitcase' are common nouns.

2) Some common nouns can also be <u>abstract nouns</u>. Abstract nouns are things you <u>can't see</u>, <u>hear</u>, <u>touch</u>, <u>smell</u> or <u>taste</u>, like <u>emotions</u> or <u>ideas</u>.

> loyalty, truth, happiness, fear ⟵ These are abstract nouns.

3) *Collective Nouns are for Groups of Things*

Remember, a collective noun isn't the same as a plural noun.

1) Collective nouns name a <u>group of things</u>.
2) They don't start with a capital letter <u>either</u>.

> A bunch of flowers.   A herd of cows.   A troop of monkeys.

'bunch', 'herd' and 'troop' are all collective nouns.

A *Pronoun* can be used *Instead* of a noun

1) Pronouns are words that you use <u>instead of nouns</u>.

2) They save you from <u>repeating</u> the <u>same noun</u> again and again.

> Ralph took his dog for a walk but it ran away from him.

← 'it' and 'him' are pronouns — they replace the nouns.

These *Pronouns* are all *Important*

Pronouns for **One Person** or **Thing**

I ⟹ me ⟹ mine
you ⟹ you ⟹ yours
he ⟹ him ⟹ his
she ⟹ her ⟹ hers
it ⟹ it ⟹ its

Pronouns for **More Than One Person** or **Thing**

we ⟹ us ⟹ ours
you ⟹ you ⟹ yours
they ⟹ them ⟹ theirs

These are possessive pronouns. They're used to show ownership.

You may be asked to *Recognise* different types of *Nouns*

Q Circle seven common nouns in the passage below.

The incompetent wizard became nervous when Emma asked him for a demonstration. "OK," he said, "I'm going to turn your hair orange." He closed his eyes and muttered the spell. The crowd of people gasped — Emma had been turned into a frog.

Method — Pick out the types of things and people

1) Work through the passage <u>one sentence</u> at a time.

2) Be careful not to circle <u>proper</u> or <u>collective</u> nouns.

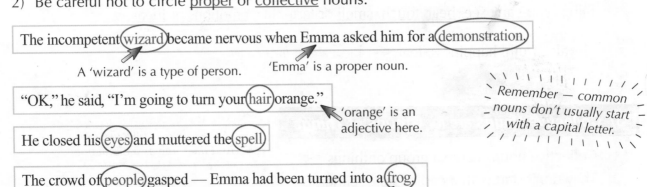

The incompetent (wizard) became nervous when Emma asked him for a (demonstration.)

A 'wizard' is a type of person.　　'Emma' is a proper noun.

"OK," he said, "I'm going to turn your (hair) orange."

'orange' is an adjective here.

He closed his (eyes) and muttered the (spell)

The crowd of (people) gasped — Emma had been turned into a (frog.)

'crowd' is a collective noun.　　A frog is a kind of animal, so it's a common noun.

Remember — common nouns don't usually start with a capital letter.

Make sure that you can **Replace a Noun** with a **Pronoun**

> **Q** Rewrite the passage below, replacing nouns with pronouns where they are needed.
>
> *PC Waddock is investigating a robbery at Mr Forde's house last Tuesday. PC Waddock knows that the robber was female, but nobody has provided any leads about the robber's identity. The robber stole a valuable vase and Mr Forde is offering a £1000 reward for the valuable vase's return.*

Method — Look for nouns that are repeated

1) Work through the passage <u>one sentence</u> at a time.
2) Look for places in the passage where the <u>same noun</u> is <u>repeated</u>.
3) Make sure that the sentence <u>still makes sense</u> when you replace the noun.

PC Waddock is investigating a robbery at Mr Forde's house last Tuesday. ← This sentence is fine. There are no repeated nouns.

PC Waddock knows that the robber was female, but nobody has provided any leads about her identity.

You can't replace 'PC Waddock' with 'he' here — it wouldn't be clear if the pronoun was referring to PC Waddock or Mr Forde.

'The robber' is repeated in this sentence. The robber is female, so change 'the robber's' to 'her'.

She stole a valuable vase and Mr Forde is offering a £1000 reward for its return.

'The robber' can be replaced by 'she' here to avoid repetition.

'Valuable vase' is repeated in this sentence. You can add 'its' here instead.

Practice Questions

1) Write down whether these words are proper nouns, common nouns or collective nouns.

   a) <u>swarm</u> of bees   d) *cauliflower*   g) <u>class</u> of children
   b) *December*   e) *lady*   h) *hockey*
   c) *Scotland*   f) *ostrich*   i) *Sue Shaw*

2) Rewrite the passage below, replacing nouns with pronouns where they are needed.

   Helen and Yasmin swam desperately towards the island in the distance, although the island wasn't getting any closer. After a while, Helen and Yasmin felt their feet touch the sandy shore and Helen and Yasmin knew that they had made it. Helen looked around and Helen saw a completely deserted paradise which had never been visited by humans before. Yasmin saw a tree heavily laden with fruit a short distance away. "Come on Helen," Yasmin said. "Let's get something to eat."

Verbs

In the sentence 'I adore treacle tart', the verb is 'adore'.

A **Verb** is a **Doing** or **Being Word**

1) Verbs are words about an <u>action</u> or <u>describing a state of being</u>.

Carl sings in the shower.	←	The verb is 'sings'.

Shirley is happy.	←	The verb is 'is'.

Every sentence has to have a verb.

2) The verb needs to <u>agree</u> with the <u>subject</u> of the sentence (the person or thing doing the action). If they don't agree, the sentence <u>won't make sense</u> (see p.4).

The **Tense** of a verb tells you **When It's Happening**

Verbs can be in the <u>past</u> tense, the <u>present</u> tense or the <u>future</u> tense.

Roberta played the lead role.	⇐ past tense ⇒	Roberta has played the lead role.

Roberta plays the lead role.	⇐ present tense ⇒	Roberta is playing the lead role.

Roberta will play the lead role.	⇐ future tense ⇒	Roberta will be playing the lead role.

Sometimes there's more than one verb making up a verb phrase.

Active and **Passive Verbs** tell you **Who** or **What**

Active Verbs tell you **Who's Doing the Action**

Most verbs in sentences are active verbs.

1) <u>Active verbs</u> make it clear <u>who's</u> doing the action.

2) The sentence is about the person or thing doing the action. The verb agrees with the <u>person</u> or <u>thing</u> that does the action (the subject).

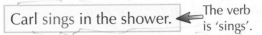 Tricia opened the parcel.

This noun is the subject.   This is the verb.

We think fighting is wrong.

This pronoun is the subject.   This is the verb.

Passive Verbs tell you **What's Being Done**

1) <u>Passive verbs</u> say <u>what's happening</u>, but they <u>don't</u> always say <u>who</u> is doing the action.

2) Passive sentences <u>focus</u> on the <u>action</u>. The <u>subject</u> can be included by adding '<u>by + subject</u>' at the end of the <u>sentence</u>, but you don't need to include it.

The parcel was opened.

The sentence doesn't tell you who opened the parcel.

It is agreed that fighting is wrong.

This sentence doesn't tell you who agreed that fighting is wrong.

A verb is made passive with the correct part of 'to be', e.g. 'was', 'is', 'are' etc.

Make sure that you can **Use Verbs** in the **Correct Tense**

 Q In each sentence, one verb has been used incorrectly.
Rewrite the sentences using the correct form of the verb.

a) "Quick, everyone *went* to your lookouts!" ordered the fireman.
b) The ball was *kick* into the back of the net.
c) My rabbit is *escape* at this very moment.
d) Yesterday, my brother *refuse* to clean his bedroom.

Method — Work out when the action is happening

a) "Quick, everyone go to your lookouts!" ordered the fireman. ◄— The fireman is issuing an instruction in the present tense. So, 'went' needs to change to 'go'.

b) The ball was kicked into the back of the net. ◄— The clue here is 'was' — it tells you that the sentence is in the past tense. So, you need to change 'kick' to 'kicked'.

c) My rabbit is escaping at this very moment. ◄— 'is' tells you that this sentence is in the present tense and it's still happening. So, you need to change 'escape' to 'escaping'.

d) Yesterday, my brother refused to clean his bedroom. ◄— The word 'Yesterday' tells you that the sentence is in the past tense. So, use 'refused' instead of 'refuse'.

 Q

Tips and Tricks for Choosing Verbs

Look at the words around the verb to help you work out the tense
of the sentence and who is doing the action.

Practice Questions

1) Underline the verb in each sentence.
   a) *The concert starts in ten minutes' time.*
   b) *We finished our fun run in record time, despite the bird costumes.*
   c) *John perfected the decorations on the birthday cake.*
   d) *I love rock-climbing in the Lake District during the summer.*
   e) *Christmas brings increased business to many toy shops.*
   f) *The steam train rushes past on its way to the coast.*

2) Circle the correct verb to complete each one.
   a) *Barney has* eating / eat / eaten *all of my popcorn.*
   b) *I have* going / been / went *to South Africa on holiday.*
   c) *Barry's knee is* hurted / hurts / hurting *after he fell over.*
   d) *You should* got / go / went *home or you'll be late.*
   e) *What time do you think you will* arriving / arrive / arrived?
   f) *The dolphin is about to* leaps / leaping / leap *out of the water.*

Adjectives, Adverbs and Prepositions

There are a few terms coming up for you to get your head around. First up is adjectives...

Adjectives are Describing Words

Adjectives describe Nouns

Adjectives tell you more about nouns.

| Luke was wearing a green jumper. |

This describes the jumper.

| The monster was huge and scary. |

These adjectives describe the monster.

Comparatives compare People or Objects

Comparatives are for comparing one thing with another thing.

| Sarah is taller than Dan. | | Elizabeth is less cheerful than Philip. |

Superlatives compare Lots of Things

Superlatives tell you which is the most, least, best or worst of a group of things or people.

| Yours is the biggest house on the street. | | Brett is the richest person I know. |

Adverbs describe Verbs

1) Adverbs tell you how, when or where an action is done.

Adverbs often end in -ly.

| The choir sings beautifully. | | The boys played football yesterday. |

This adverb tells you how they sing.

This adverb tells you when they played football.

2) Adverbs can also describe adjectives. They're words like 'very', 'quite' and 'totally'.

| Tracy is quite happy to go. | | The theatre is totally full. |

Prepositions tell you the Relation between Nouns or Pronouns

1) Prepositions are words like 'under', 'in front of', 'between' and 'with'.
They tell you how things are related in terms of location or space.

| Dennis sat under the bridge. | | Oliver climbed into the car. |

2) Prepositions can also tell you when things are.

| Make sure you get there before 7 pm. | | You can only play until five o'clock. |

Section One — Grammar

You might have to **Identify Parts of Speech**

> **Q** Circle the adverbs in the passage below.
>
> *With millions of tourists each year, Paris is easily one of the most popular cities on Earth. Some of the attractions that are hugely popular are the Eiffel Tower, Arc de Triomphe and Louvre Museum. Paris is famous for its beautifully maintained gardens and award-winning food.*

Method — Look for descriptions of verbs or adjectives

1) Work through the passage <u>one sentence</u> at a time.
2) Look for places in a sentence where <u>verbs</u> or <u>adjectives</u> are <u>described</u>.

> With millions of tourists each year, Paris is (easily) one of the most popular cities on Earth.

'easily' is an adverb — it changes the verb 'is'.

> Some of the attractions that are (hugely) popular are the Eiffel Tower, Arc de Triomphe and Louvre Museum.

'hugely' is describing the adjective 'popular' — it's an adverb.

> Paris is famous for its (beautifully) maintained gardens and award-winning food.

'beautifully' is describing how the gardens have been maintained. It's an adverb.

'award-winning' is not an adverb. It's describing 'food', which is a noun.

Tips and Tricks for Spotting Adverbs

Find the adjectives and verbs in a sentence first and then look to see if any other words alter their meaning — these are adverbs.

Practice Questions

1) Write down whether each option is a comparative, a superlative or just an adjective.

   a) *funnier*
   b) *strangest*
   c) *most graceful*
   d) *bizarre*
   e) *joyful*
   f) *less fascinating*

2) Underline the word in each sentence which matches the part of speech in brackets.
   a) *Chris closed his eyes nervously as the shuttle started to move.* (adverb)
   b) *Joyce leant over to tell Anupreet to try the crispy potato skins.* (adjective)
   c) *Molly looked around the side of the lorry to check for traffic.* (preposition)
   d) *I was the only child waiting to be collected after school.* (adjective)
   e) *Carrie gladly accepted the offer of a place to stay.* (adverb)
   f) *When Mum shouted at Terry, he crawled under the table to sulk.* (preposition)

Connectives

Connectives are like glue — they join different parts of a text together.

Connectives Join Clauses and Sentences

1) Connectives join <u>clauses</u> together in a <u>sentence</u>.

> I haven't got my homework because my dog ate it.

> It was raining so Mohammed put up his umbrella.

Using connectives in this way makes compound or complex sentences (see page 5).

2) Connectives can also link <u>sentences</u> together in a <u>text</u>.

> The plans for the town centre gardens will certainly bring more tourists to the town. On the other hand, more tourists will mean an increase in traffic coming into town. Furthermore, the new gardens will cost the council a lot of money.

'On the other hand' introduces a different point of view.

'Furthermore' adds to this point of view.

You'll see connectives used like this a lot in letters and newspaper articles.

Connectives can be Words or Short Phrases

Connectives may be Short Words

These short words are also called 'conjunctions'.

These are words like '<u>so</u>', '<u>if</u>', '<u>and</u>', '<u>but</u>', '<u>while</u>' and '<u>since</u>'.

> Mum's going to do some baking and she would like you to help.

> Let's go for a walk today while the weather is nice.

Connectives may be Compound Words

1) <u>Compound words</u> are made from two smaller words <u>joined together</u>.
2) These are words like '<u>however</u>', '<u>moreover</u>', '<u>whereas</u>' and '<u>meanwhile</u>'.

> Julie wanted to go to the shops, whereas I wanted to go swimming.
> However, the swimming pool was closed so our decision was made for us.

Connectives may be Short Phrases

These are phrases like '<u>because of</u>', '<u>on the other hand</u>', '<u>in other words</u>' and '<u>as a result</u>'.

> Wally wasn't sure where the exit was. In other words, he was lost.

> Nadine had left her homework at home. As a result, her teacher put her in detention.

You need to **Know How to Use Connectives**

> **Q** Circle the most appropriate connective to complete each sentence.
>
> a) *Jack's new puppy was a bundle of energy* because / but / furthermore / so *it certainly wasn't house-trained.*
>
> b) *My bus was late again today* although / therefore / also / because *the driver had called in sick.*
>
> c) *I'm really looking forward to the disco tonight* because / so / although / in case *I don't know what to wear.*

Method — Look for the meaning of the sentence

1) Look for the <u>relationship</u> between the <u>two clauses</u> in each sentence. This gives the sentence its <u>meaning</u>.

2) Choose the best <u>connective</u> that fits the meaning of the sentence.

> a) Jack's new puppy was a bundle of energy but it certainly wasn't house-trained.

The first clause gives a positive description of Jack's new puppy... ... whilst the second clause introduces a negative point. So 'but' is the most logical connective to use.

> b) My bus was late again today because the driver had called in sick.

The first clause explains that the bus was late... ... and the second clause explains why. So use 'because' to introduce the explanation.

> c) I'm really looking forward to the disco tonight although I don't know what to wear.

The first clause is a positive statement... ... but the second clause makes a negative point. 'although' is the most logical connective to use.

Practice Questions

1) Underline the connectives in the passage below.

The Amazon Rainforest covers 40% of South America, although it has decreased in size. Humans have cut down the trees because they need wood for construction and space for farms and roads. However, conservation efforts are under way to protect the rainforest and stop people from illegally cutting down the trees.

2) Circle the most appropriate connective to complete each sentence.

a) *I really like to eat cereal for breakfast.* Surely, / As a result, / Therefore, / However, *I sometimes eat a slice of toast.*

b) *I'd like to go out to the Italian restaurant tonight,* although / therefore / because / so *Chinese is my favourite.*

c) *We went to play hockey,* whenever / although / despite / besides *the rain.*

Answering Grammar Questions

These pages cover the type of grammar questions that might crop up on the Multiple Choice paper.

Multiple Choice — finding the **Best Word** to **Fit**

1) Some grammar questions will ask you to choose a <u>word or phrase</u> to complete a sentence.

2) For each line, you'll be asked to <u>choose the option</u> that is correct and makes sense.

3) It might look like this:

In the test, the passages will be about 8-10 lines long.

> **Q** In the passage below you need to choose the word, or group of words, which fits best and completes the sentence. The passage needs to make sense and be written in correct English. Mark the letter for the option you pick on your answer sheet.
>
> 1 **There is   There are   They're   There's   Their** plans to build a new supermarket in
>   A   B   C   D   E
>
> 2 Marchead town centre. The local shops **don't   do   may   have   did** suffer as more
>   A   B   C   D   E
>
> 3 people use the supermarket. **Moreover   And   However   In other words   Because**
>   A   B   C   D   E
>
> 4 a final decision won't be made until a meeting with local residents on Monday.

Method — Read through the whole sentence carefully

Read each sentence to yourself, testing each option <u>one at a time</u>.

1) You need to select the <u>correct introduction</u> for the <u>first</u> sentence:

> There are plans to build a new supermarket in Marchead town centre.

'There are' is the correct option.
'plans' is plural so you need to use
'There are' instead of 'There is' or 'There's'.

'There are' is option B, so you'd mark 'B' on your answer sheet.

You'll need to look at the whole sentence to work out the answer.

2) The <u>second</u> sentence looks at a <u>possible</u> impact of the supermarket:

> The local shops may suffer as more people use the supermarket.

The shops have not already suffered and it is not certain that they will.
The correct option to use is 'may' — option C.

3) You need to choose the <u>correct connective</u> at the beginning of the third sentence:

> However, a final decision won't be made until a meeting with local residents on Monday.

There is a change in tone in this sentence.
'However' is the correct connective to use — option C.

All of the other options would be used to expand on the point in the last sentence.

Multiple Choice — answering Comprehension Questions

1) You may be asked grammar questions as part of your comprehension test.
   These questions will be about the way words or phrases are used in the passage.

2) You'll need to be able to identify specific parts of speech, but you'll be given options
   to choose from (see Section Five for more on comprehension questions).

Q Read the passage and then answer the following questions.

1   *Before I was two years old, a circumstance happened which I have never forgotten.*
    It was early in the spring; there had been a little frost in the night, and a light mist
    still hung over the plantations and meadows. I and the other colts were feeding at
    the lower part of the field when we heard, quite in the distance, what sounded like
5   *the cry of dogs. The oldest of the colts raised his head, pricked his ears, and said,*
    "There are the hounds!" and immediately cantered off followed by the rest of us to
    the upper part of the field, where we could look over the hedge and see several
    fields beyond. My mother and an old riding horse of our master's were also
    standing near, and seemed to know all about it.

    From 'Black Beauty' by Anna Sewell

1) What type of word is 'colts' (lines 3 and 5)?

   A Adjective   **B** Preposition   **C** Noun   **D** Adverb   **E** Pronoun

2) What type of word is 'immediately' (line 6)?

   A Preposition   **B** Adverb   **C** Collective noun   **D** Adjective   **E** Verb

3) Which of these words is a preposition: *'It was early in the spring'* (line 2)?

   A It   **B** was   **C** early   **D** in   **E** spring

Method — Look for evidence in the text

1) To answer question 1, read the surrounding text to see how the word 'colts' is used:

   > I and the other colts were feeding at the lower part of the field...

   These extracts help you to work out that the colts are animals. The word 'colts' must therefore be a noun — option C.

   > The oldest of the colts raised his head, pricked his ears...

2) Do the same for question 2. Look at how the word 'immediately' is used:

   > ... and immediately cantered off...

   'cantered' is a verb, so 'immediately' is an adverb because it's describing how the action was done — option B.

3) Question 3 is a bit different — you only need to look at the words in the question.

   > It was early in the spring

   A preposition shows how things are related, usually in terms of time and place. In this case, the preposition is 'in' — option D.

Answering Grammar Questions

These pages should help you to get your head around Standard Answer grammar questions.

Standard Answer — answering Comprehension Questions

These questions are just like Multiple Choice comprehension questions, but there won't be any options to choose from — you'll have to pick out the correct parts of speech yourself.

Q Read the passage below and then answer the questions that follow.

1   The door led right into a large kitchen, which was full of smoke from one end to the other: the Duchess was sitting on a three-legged stool in the middle, nursing a baby: the cook was leaning over the fire, stirring a large cauldron which seemed to be full of soup.

5   "There's certainly too much pepper in that soup!" Alice said to herself, as well as she could for sneezing.

There was certainly too much of it in the air. Even the Duchess sneezed occasionally; and as for the baby, it was sneezing and howling alternately without a moment's pause. The only two creatures in the kitchen, that did not sneeze, were

10   the cook, and a large cat, which was lying on the hearth and grinning from ear to ear.

"Please would you tell me," said Alice, a little timidly, for she was not quite sure whether it was good manners for her to speak first, "why your cat grins like that?"

"It's a Cheshire-Cat," said the Duchess, "and that's why. Pig!"

15   She said the last word with such sudden violence that Alice quite jumped; but she saw in another moment that it was addressed to the baby, and not to her, so she took courage, and went on again: —

"I didn't know that Cheshire-Cats always grinned; in fact, I didn't know that cats could grin."

"They all can," said the Duchess; "and most of 'em do."

From 'Alice's Adventures in Wonderland' by Lewis Carroll

1) Give one example of each of the following parts of speech in this sentence taken from the passage.

"Please would you tell me," said Alice, a little timidly, for she was not quite sure whether it was good manners for her to speak first, "why your cat grins like that?"

a) a proper noun   c) a common noun

b) a connective   d) an adverb

2) Who is the pronoun 'she' referring to in line 15?

3) Is the verb in 'it was addressed to the baby' (line 16) active or passive?
Explain your answer.

Think about how to spot *Parts of Speech*

Method — Read the text very carefully

1) To answer question 1, look carefully for each <u>part of speech</u>:

'Alice' is the only proper noun in the sentence. So 'Alice' is the answer to part a).

'timidly', 'not', 'quite' and 'first' are adverbs because they describe verbs or adjectives.

"Please would you tell me," said Alice, a little timidly, for she was not quite sure whether it was good manners for her to speak first, "why your cat grins like that?"

'whether' is a connective — it could answer part b).

'manners' and 'cat' are the only two common nouns in this sentence. Either could be the answer to part c).

'for' is another connective in this sentence — it continues the sentence and explains why Alice spoke timidly. It could be the answer to part b).

2) For question 2, look at the <u>line before</u> line 15 to work out <u>who</u> is speaking.

"It's a Cheshire-Cat," said the Duchess, "and that's why. Pig!"

She said the last word with such sudden violence that Alice quite jumped;

The Duchess is speaking here, so it is the Duchess being referred to as 'she' in line 15.

Be careful — Alice is the only character named in the line, so you could be tricked into thinking that 'she' refers to her.

3) To work out whether 'it was addressed' is <u>active</u> or <u>passive</u>, read the text around it.

she saw in another moment that it was addressed to the baby

The verb is focusing on the action, rather than the person doing it, so the sentence is passive.

Practice Questions

1) Read the passage below and then answer the questions that follow.

1 *Harriet was desperate not to be distracted again. She'd already been trying to do*
2 *her Maths homework for two hours and she had to get it finished before she could*
3 *go out and play. However, she could hear an incessant buzzing noise, and it was*
4 *really putting her off. Angrily, she hauled herself to her feet and started to search*
5 *her bedroom for the culprit. The noise was coming from near the window...*

   a) Find a connective used in line 3 of the passage.

   b) What part of speech is 'desperate' (line 1)?

   c) What part of speech is 'angrily' (line 4)?

✳ Stop 2

Starting and Ending Sentences

Sentences can be tricky to understand when punctuation marks are missing.

Warm-Up Activity

In a book or magazine that you're reading:

1) Find <u>three sentences</u> that end with "?"
2) Try to find a sentence that ends with "!" or "..." — there won't be as many of those.

Start each sentence with a *Capital Letter*...

For the start of a sentence, there's just one very simple rule.
Whatever you ended the last sentence with, always <u>start</u> the next with a <u>capital letter</u>.

> My friend Holly loves the summer. She always eats ice cream.

capital letter at the start　　　　　　　another capital letter for a new sentence

...*End* with a *Full Stop*, *Exclamation Mark*, *Question Mark* or *Ellipsis*

You've got <u>four options</u> at the <u>end</u> of a sentence.
You need to learn when and how to use each one...

● **A *Full Stop* goes at the end of a *Statement***

If you're just writing an <u>ordinary statement</u>, use a full stop.

> Sam put the parcel up to his ear and shook it gently. It rattled.

another full stop

a full stop

! An *Exclamation Mark* shows *Strong Feelings*

1) Use an exclamation mark to show strong feelings like <u>fear</u>, <u>anger</u> or <u>surprise</u>.

> Ouch, that was my foot!

This exclamation mark shows shock and pain.

2) Exclamation marks can also show someone <u>shouting</u> or giving a <u>command</u>.

> Don't run!

This exclamation mark shows a command.

Try not to use too many exclamation marks in your writing. It makes you sound over the top.

? **A Question Mark** *goes at the end of a* **Question**

1) Question marks are only for sentences that actually <u>ask</u> a question.

> What time is it**?** ← You need a question mark here.

2) Don't put them at the end of sentences that just tell you <u>about</u> a question.

> She asked what time it was**.** ← **no** question mark here

• • • **An** *Ellipsis* *leaves a sentence* **Hanging**

1) If you want to deliberately leave a sentence <u>unfinished</u>, you can use an ellipsis (three dots). This can be good for adding <u>suspense</u> to a story.

> It had seemed like such a good idea, but**...** ← This ellipsis could be used at the end of a chapter to add suspense.

2) They're also a good way to show <u>interrupted speech</u>.

> "Rachael! Er, I was just**...**"

You might be asked to **Split Up** a passage into **Sentences**

> **Q** This paragraph is missing full stops and capital letters.
> Rewrite the passage so that it is correctly split into sentences.
>
> *tigers, lions and cheetahs are all part of the big cat family tigers live in Asia, and are jungle animals lions and cheetahs both live on the plains of Africa*

Method — Where you take a big breath, put a full stop

1) You know that the first word is the <u>start</u> of a sentence, so it needs a <u>capital T</u>.
2) Now read the passage through (aloud if that helps) and put in a full stop and capital letter each time you take a <u>big breath</u>. This is where you start a new point.

capital letter at the start   big breath

> **T**igers, lions and cheetahs are all part of the big cat family**.** **T**igers live in Asia, and are jungle animals**.** **L**ions and cheetahs both live on the plains of Africa**.**

big breath

Don't forget the full stop at the end.

You should also be able to *Spot Mistakes* in a passage

Q In this passage there are some mistakes in the use of capital letters and punctuation. On each numbered line there is either one mistake or no mistake. Draw a circle around each mistake.

1 *"Let's go to Millom" cried Sammy excitedly.*
2 *Harry sighed because they always went to Millom on Sammy's birthday.*
3 *"Are you sure?" asked Harry. "wouldn't you rather go to Windermere?"*

Method — Check the passage line by line

1) Line 1 has speech showing <u>strong emotion</u>, so it should have an <u>exclamation mark</u>.

"Let's go to Millom" cried Sammy excitedly.   *See p.28 for rules on writing speech.*

2) There are <u>no mistakes</u> in Line 2. It starts with a capital letter and ends with a full stop. And it doesn't have anything fancy, like speech, to catch you out.

3) Line 3 has <u>two sentences</u> in it, so check each sentence separately:

"Are you sure?" asked Harry. ◄—— This bit's fine...

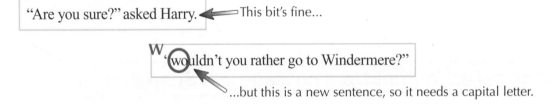

"wouldn't you rather go to Windermere?"

...but this is a new sentence, so it needs a capital letter.

Practice Questions

1) Rewrite these sentences, adding the correct punctuation to start and end each one.
   a) look out — it's the mutant cheesecake   b) does this hat make my ears look funny

2) Write a sentence to show the correct use of:
   a) an ellipsis.   b) a question mark.   c) an exclamation mark.   d) a full stop.

3) In this passage there are some mistakes in the use of capital letters and punctuation. Each line has one mistake or no mistakes. Rewrite the passage with no mistakes.
   1 *Peter Handy was a fisherman. Every day he went out on his boat in the bay to*
   2 *catch fish. One day he went down to the dock as usual to find his boat missing?*
   3 *"Oh dear!" cried Peter. "What am I going to do now?"*
   4 *He sat down on the dock and put his head in his hands. But just then?*

Commas, Dashes and Brackets

Some sentences, like this one, sound a lot better if commas are used correctly.

Warm-Up Activity

Write a <u>list</u> of all the different <u>types of biscuit</u> you can think of. See if you can work out <u>where</u> you should add the <u>commas</u>. Try to get as many biscuits as possible:

<u>5 biscuits</u> — biscuit novice   <u>10 biscuits</u> — biscuit expert   <u>15 biscuits</u> — biscuit pro

Commas *Separate* parts of a *Sentence*

Here are <u>three examples</u> of when you should use a comma in a sentence:

A comma *Separates Items* in a *List*

1) A list that <u>doesn't</u> contain any commas is <u>really hard</u> to understand.

I love ice cream cake sandwiches and chips.

2) Put a comma <u>after</u> each item in the list to break up the sentence:

I love ice cream, cake, sandwiches and chips.

Add commas here.

Put 'and' or 'or' between the last two items in a list. Remember, you don't need to use a comma before 'and' or 'or'.

A comma *Separates Clauses* in a *Sentence*

1) This sentence contains <u>two clauses</u>. They're joined together using 'but'.

Amir went swimming on Saturday but I decided to stay at home.

1st clause   2nd clause

There's more about clauses on pages 4 and 5.

2) Adding a comma <u>separates</u> the two clauses. This makes the sentence easier to read.

Amir went swimming on Saturday, but I decided to stay at home.

You put the comma after the first clause.

A comma *Adds Information* to a *Sentence*

1) When a sentence contains <u>extra information</u>, you need to separate it using a <u>comma</u> so that the sentence <u>makes sense</u>.

With a scream Hayley turned on the light.

It feels like there should be a natural pause in the sentence here.

2) A comma <u>separates</u> the extra information from the main sentence.

With a scream, Hayley turned on the light.

It's now clear that Hayley is screaming as she turns on the light.

Section Two — Punctuation

Brackets and Dashes also Separate Information

Brackets bring Extra Information into a sentence

Add <u>brackets around</u> extra information to keep it separate:

> My friend Zara is really good at football (she's a striker).

You don't need to know this to understand the sentence.

> Carly and Adam (who are both 14) are going shopping.

Brackets should always be used in pairs.

Dashes can be used Instead of Brackets

Dashes can be used in pairs or on their own.

1) You can add <u>a pair of dashes</u> around extra information to keep it <u>separate</u>.

> The best thing my mum can cook — if she can cook anything — is beans on toast.

2) <u>Single dashes</u> can mark a <u>pause</u> that's <u>longer</u> than a <u>comma</u>.

> I peered into the shed and there it was on a shelf — Mary's old violin.

This dash shows a longer pause.

You might see dashes used in dialogue.

You might be asked to Add Punctuation to a Passage

Q This extract is missing some punctuation. Rewrite the extract, adding commas, dashes and brackets where they are needed.

Julie Mia and Rory were going to the airport they were flying to Madrid. Rory was scared of flying so he was feeling very nervous. Smugly Julie told him to stop being so pathetic.

Method — Check for lists, clauses and extra information

1) The first sentence has a <u>list</u> and <u>extra information</u> which need to be <u>separated</u>:

> Julie, Mia and Rory were going to the airport (they were flying to Madrid).

Comma needed here to break up the list.

A pair of brackets (or a dash) is needed here.

2) The second sentence has <u>two clauses</u> that need to be separated by a <u>comma</u>:

> Rory was scared of flying, so he was feeling very nervous.

1st clause   comma   2nd clause

3) '<u>Smugly</u>' is extra information in the third sentence that needs a <u>comma</u>:

> Smugly, Julie told him to stop being so pathetic.

The commas in the second and third sentences represent short pauses in the way they would be spoken.

Some questions may ask you to *Spot Punctuation Errors*

 Q Circle the errors in the use of commas and brackets in the passage below.

> 1 *Max was desperate, to visit the zoo at half-term (he had never been before).*
> 2 *He really wanted to see the lions, giraffes, tigers, and monkeys.*
> 3 *When he arrived at 4pm it was a long drive Max heard that the tiger was ill.*

Method — Read each sentence out to yourself

1) Start by reading Line 1 aloud. There is <u>extra punctuation</u> that shouldn't be there.

> Max was desperate, to visit the zoo at half-term (he had never been before).

This comma is wrong — the pause isn't needed.   The brackets are right — they separate the information.

2) Then move on to Line 2. <u>Not every item</u> in the list needs a <u>comma</u> after it:

> He really wanted to see the lions, giraffes, tigers, and monkeys.

These two commas are right — they split up the list.   This comma is not needed.

3) Then read out Line 3. This one is different — it needs <u>punctuation adding</u> to it:

> When he arrived at 4pm (it was a long drive), Max heard that the tiger was ill.

Brackets separate the extra information.   A comma is needed after the bracket to separate the clauses in the sentence.

Practice Questions

1) Rewrite each sentence, adding one comma to make each one correct.
   a) *Subia didn't want to go fishing with her dad but he'd brought the equipment.*
   b) *Ravens pigeons and seagulls were Nicci's least favourite types of bird.*
   c) *Albert ran for his train but he was already four minutes late.*
   d) *Although they couldn't hear George shouted angrily at the boys as they ran away.*

> *Each bracket in the pair counts as one error.*

2) There are ten errors in the use of commas and brackets in the passage below. Rewrite the paragraph using the correct punctuation.

Gareth, and Lucy were sick of their P.E. teacher Mr Oden. Every day he made them do high jump, shot-put, rugby (and football). One day they came up with a cunning plan along with the other children to get revenge on Mr Oden. They took all of the studs out, of his football boots they stole them from under his desk so that when he put them on and started running he fell head first into the mud.

Apostrophes

It's easy to get muddled with apostrophes — luckily these pages explain what you need to know.

Warm-Up Activity

Write as many sentences as you can that use at least two of the words below.

wouldn't   Julia's   I'm   hadn't   it's   you're

Apostrophes *show* Possession...

1) When you're writing about who owns what, add an <u>apostrophe</u> to the <u>noun</u>:

My dog**'s** dinner	My dogs**'** dinner	The children**'s** dinner

The noun is singular (there's one dog). Add an apostrophe + 's'.

The noun is plural and ends in 's' (there's more than one dog). Add an apostrophe after the 's'.

The noun is plural but doesn't end in 's'. Add an apostrophe + 's'.

There are other common plural nouns that don't end in 's' — e.g. 'men', 'women' and 'people'.

2) When the noun is a <u>name</u>, just add an <u>apostrophe + 's'</u>:

Zuzanna**'s** dog	James**'s** car

...*and where a* Short Form *has been made*

Apostrophes *show* Short Forms

1) Apostrophes are used to make <u>short forms</u> of words.

2) You add an apostrophe where <u>letters</u> have been <u>removed</u>.

We**'**re all off on holiday. ← When you write 'we're' instead of 'we are', the apostrophe shows where 'a' has been left out.

3) Here's a list of common short forms:

I am	⇒	I'm
I will not	⇒	I won't
I would	⇒	I'd
I had	⇒	I'd
I have	⇒	I've

they are	⇒	they're
who is	⇒	who's
do not	⇒	don't
does not	⇒	doesn't
can not	⇒	can't

It's *is the* Short Form *of* It Is *or* It Has

If you're not sure whether to use 'its' or 'it's', ask yourself whether the sentence would make sense if it said 'it is' or 'it has' instead.

1) '<u>It's</u>' with an apostrophe is always short for '<u>it is</u>' or '<u>it has</u>'.

It's raining outside.	← It is raining outside.

It's been raining for days.	← It has been raining for days.

2) '<u>Its</u>' means something <u>belongs to it</u>. It <u>never</u> has an apostrophe.

Have you fed the dog its dinner?	The team has won its match.

Make sure that you can **Add Apostrophes** to **Text**

Q This extract is missing some apostrophes. Rewrite the extract, adding the apostrophes where they are needed.

1 *Michelles horse is called George and its amazing how lazy he is.*
2 *Hes always looking for food and he wont move a muscle if its been raining.*
3 *Georges vet is going to do some tests to make sure that he isnt ill.*

Method — Look for possession and short forms of words

Read through <u>each line</u>. Look closely for places where apostrophes <u>may be needed</u>.

Michelle's horse is called George and it's amazing how lazy he is.

An apostrophe is needed here — the horse belongs to Michelle.

This is the short form of 'it is', so add an apostrophe here.

He's always looking for food and he won't move a muscle if it's been raining.

This is short for 'he is'. Add an apostrophe here.

This is the short form of 'will not'.

Add an apostrophe here — this means 'it has'.

George's vet is going to do some tests to make sure that he isn't ill.

Add an apostrophe here. The vet belongs to George.

'tests' is a plural noun so you don't need an apostrophe here.

This is the short form of 'is not', so add an apostrophe here.

Practice Questions

1) These sentences are each missing an apostrophe.
   Rewrite the sentences, adding the apostrophes where they are needed.

   a) *Megan's goalkeeper jersey wasnt going to dry in time for her match.*
   b) *"There's no way that you're going out when its this cold," shouted Zac's mum.*
   c) *Marcos new computer game was taking its time to arrive.*
   d) *Beatrice suddenly realised that she'd left her homework at her dads house.*
   e) *The policemens boots were covered in mud from the garden.*

2) The passage below contains four errors in the use of apostrophes.
   Write it out again with the correct apostrophes.

   Freds room was definitely haunted. Every night he could hear a ghostly whistling coming from inside his wardrobe. One night, the wardrobe door started to rock noisily on it's base. Fred leapt out of bed and called for his' mum to come and investigate the wardrobe. She slowly opened the door to reveal Fred's sister hiding inside. "That wasnt funny," yelled Fred, as his sister rolled around laughing on the floor.

Speech

There's nothing scary about speech marks — you just have to use them in the right places.

Warm-Up Activity

Watch a clip of your <u>favourite film</u> for <u>30 seconds</u>.
Write down what is being <u>said</u>. See if you can use <u>speech marks</u> in the right places.
For example, "Quick! Call the police!" shouted Fran. "The robber is getting away!"

Speech Marks *show when someone is* **Speaking**

1) You need to use <u>speech marks</u> when you quote the <u>actual words</u> that <u>someone speaks</u>.

2) The speech marks go <u>before</u> and <u>after</u> the spoken words.

> "Are you sure this is the right way, Mick?" asked Judith.

Speech marks go at the start and end of the speech.

3) You should <u>only</u> use speech marks if you quote <u>exactly</u> what someone has said.

> Judith asked Mick if he was sure that it was the right way.

There's no actual speech in this sentence, so you don't need speech marks.

This is called indirect speech or reported speech— you don't know exactly what was said.

Speech *always ends with a* **Punctuation Mark**

There are <u>four rules</u> that you need to learn:

1) Use a **Comma** if the **Sentence Continues** after the speech ends

> "Let's go on the roller coaster," suggested Dwayne.

The sentence continues after the speech, so add a comma.

2) Use a **Full Stop** if the **Sentence Ends** when the speech ends

> Harry said, "I'd love to go hiking."

The sentence ends here, so you need a full stop.
This comma introduces the speech.

3) Use an **Exclamation Mark** if the speech shows **Strong Feelings**

> "Tidy your room!" yelled Sam.

Sam is shouting, so it needs an exclamation mark.

4) Use a **Question Mark** if the speech is a **Question**

> "Where are you going?" asked Alia.

This is a question, so it needs a question mark.

You may have to **Add Speech Marks** to **Text**

 Q Rewrite this passage, adding speech marks where they are needed.

1 Mum, can we get a puppy? asked Laura, for the sixth time that week.
2 Laura's mum sighed, Who would take it for a walk?
3 Laura spent the next five minutes telling her mum how she'd have time to do it.

Method — Look for quoted speech in the passage

1) Work through the passage <u>one sentence</u> at a time.

2) Make sure that you only add speech marks to words that <u>someone has said</u>.

> "Mum, can we get a puppy?" asked Laura, for the sixth time that week.

These are the actual words Laura says
to her mum, so they need speech marks.

> Laura's mum sighed, "Who would take it for a walk?"

Laura's mum is asking a question
here, so this needs speech marks.

3) Remember that you <u>don't</u> need speech marks for <u>reported speech</u>.

> Laura spent the next five minutes telling her mum how she'd have time to do it.

This isn't Laura's actual
speech, so it doesn't
need speech marks.

Tips and Tricks for Using Speech Marks

Make sure that you put the correct bits of punctuation inside the speech marks. If the speech is a question or exclamation, you'll need to put the question mark or exclamation mark inside the speech marks.

Practice Questions

1) Write down the sentence in each pair that has been punctuated correctly.
   a) *"Listen carefully," said Matt, as he told them about the "wizard's warning".* OR
      "Listen carefully," said Matt, as he told them about the wizard's warning.
   b) *Alex screamed into the night air, "Why can't I find the way"?* OR
      Alex screamed into the night air, "Why can't I find the way?"
   c) *I need "three starters, two desserts and one drink," shouted the waiter.* OR
      "I need three starters, two desserts and one drink," shouted the waiter.

2) The sentences below are missing speech marks.
   Rewrite the sentences, adding speech marks where they are needed.

   a) *How many people are coming? asked Giles.*
   b) *Helen asked, Will you have time to visit Maggie, George? I'm too busy.*
   c) *Take some sun cream! shouted Heidi. It's sweltering out there.*

Section Two — Punctuation

Colons and Semicolons

You're nearly there for punctuation — just colons and semicolons left to learn.

Warm-Up Activity

Look in a <u>newspaper</u> or a <u>magazine</u>. See if you can find three sentences that use a <u>colon</u> ":" and three sentences that use a <u>semicolon</u> ";".

Colons *and* Semicolons Add Information *to* Sentences

Colons *Introduce* Lists *and* Explanations

1) You can use a <u>colon</u> to show that a <u>list</u> is about to begin:

> You will need the following equipment: tennis racket, tennis balls, T-shirt, shorts, socks and trainers.

The colon goes here, just before the list begins.

2) You can also use a <u>colon</u> to introduce an <u>explanation</u> in a sentence:

> The office was empty: everyone had finished work and gone home.

Add a colon here, before the explanation.

This is the explanation — it's explaining why the office was empty.

Semicolons *Join Clauses and* Break Up Lists

1) <u>Semicolons</u> are used to join <u>two sentences</u> into <u>one</u>. The sentences must be about the <u>same thing</u>, and they must both contain a <u>main clause</u>.

There's more about clauses on page 4.

> You're going to see him tomorrow; you'll know more then.

The semicolon joins the two sentences together.

The sentences could also be joined using a connective (see p. 14).

2) <u>Semicolons</u> are also used to break up lists of <u>long phrases or clauses</u>.

> In 2008, the fête had stalls selling cakes; in 2009, there was a 'guess the number of sweets in the jar' competition; and in 2010, the local children danced round a maypole.

You need a semicolon before the 'and'.

Colons *and* Semicolons *are used* Differently

Remember that a <u>colon</u> offers an <u>explanation</u> of what comes before it, but a semicolon doesn't.

> Liam is happy; George has baked a cake.

The semicolon implies that the two clauses are related — it suggests that Liam's happiness and George's baking might have the same cause or that the two things happened at the same time.

> Liam is happy: George has baked a cake.

The colon shows that Liam is happy because George has baked a cake.

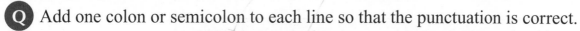

Learn how to **Add Colons** and **Semicolons** to **Sentences**

> **Q** Add one colon or semicolon to each line so that the punctuation is correct.
>
> a) *Here's what you need 4 eggs, 300 g of flour and 200 g of sugar.*
> b) *Kyle is on holiday this week German class will go ahead as usual.*
> c) *Mr Smith was furious I'd forgotten my homework again.*

Method — Find lists, clauses and explanations

1) Find the <u>place</u> in each sentence where a colon or semicolon <u>could be added</u>.
2) Don't <u>confuse</u> colons and semicolons — take a look back at the <u>last page</u> if you're not sure.

a) Here's what you need**:** 4 eggs, 300 g of flour and 200 g of sugar.

A colon goes here, before the start of the list of ingredients.

The items in this list are short phrases, so you use a colon and not a semicolon.

b) Kyle is on holiday this week**;** German class will go ahead as usual.

The two clauses are related, but the second clause isn't an explanation or a definition. So you need to use a semicolon.

c) Mr Smith was furious**:** I'd forgotten my homework again.

Add a colon here.

This part of the sentence explains why Mr Smith was furious.

Practice Questions

1) There are three errors in the use of colons and semicolons in this passage. Find the errors and write the passage out again.

Pierre was very excited: it was the end of term. He was going to Greece on holiday the very next day. Pierre was looking forward to swimming in the bright blue sea: browsing the local Greek markets, looking for souvenirs; playing tennis at the hotel and paying a visit to Athens. He didn't want to go to any museums: his mum would probably make him go anyway.

2) Each of these sentences is missing at least one semicolon. Rewrite each sentence and add the missing semicolons.

You may need to add more than one semicolon to the sentences.

a) *I've worked really hard I expect to pass my exams.*
b) *I never miss a football match I'm the top scorer in the team.*
c) *I went to the market for a new hat, but they didn't have any I'll be back on Monday.*
d) *I would like to thank my mum, who inspired me to sing my teacher, who taught me how to hit the high notes and my partner, who wrote me some great songs.*

Answering Punctuation Questions

Questions in the real test can be a punctuation minefield — these pages will help you answer them.

Multiple Choice — finding punctuation mistakes

1) If you're taking a <u>Multiple Choice</u> paper, you might get a question asking you to <u>find</u> the punctuation <u>mistakes</u> in a short passage.

2) For each line, you'll be asked to <u>identify</u> if there's a mistake; and if there is, you'll need to say <u>where</u> in the line the mistake is.

3) It might look a bit like this:

In the test, the passages will be about 8-10 lines long.

Q There are some punctuation errors in this passage. In each line there is either one mistake or no mistake. Find the group of words with the mistake in it and mark its letter on your answer sheet. If there is no mistake, mark N.

1 Will you do something amazing today? Please read on to learn more. Drought

   A   B   C   D N

2 victims in Africa desperately need food; clean water and other essential items.

   A   B   C   D N

3 Any money (no matter how little) can make a difference. Please help us?

   A   B   C   D N

You'll mark A, B, C, D or N on your answer sheet.

You'll need to Read the Passage Carefully

Method — Check the passage line by line

Read the passage through <u>once</u> before you <u>write</u> anything, then read it <u>line by line</u>. Check that the punctuation in the line is <u>correct</u>, then check if any punctuation is <u>missing</u>.

1) Line 1 has <u>no mistakes</u> in it, so the answer is N.

2) Line 2 looks <u>fairly simple</u> until you get to the middle of the line where there's a <u>semicolon</u>.

> victims in Africa desperately need food**;** clean water and other essential items.

The mistake is in part B — the list contains short items, so they don't need to be separated by a semicolon. Use a comma instead.

3) Line 3 has <u>two sentences</u> that you need to check.

> Any money (no matter how little) can make a difference. Please help us**?**

This sentence is fine.

This is an appeal for help, not a question. It's wrong to use a question mark here, so the answer is D.

Standard Answer — adding the **Correct Punctuation**

1) If you're taking a <u>Standard Answer</u> paper, your question will be slightly different.

2) You'll be given a <u>passage</u> with <u>mistakes</u> in (or <u>no punctuation</u> at all) which you'll need to rewrite with the <u>correct punctuation</u>. It might look a bit like this:

> **Q** Add the missing punctuation to the passage below.
>
> *Charlotte was furious with Ronald her next-door neighbour he kept shouting at the top of his voice playing loud music and kicking footballs against her bedroom window she opened her window one day caught the football and refused to give it back you can have it back when you learn to grow up she shouted.*
>
> *(10 marks)*

Use the number of marks as a guide, but remember that there's usually more than one mistake per mark.

You'll need to *Think* about *What's Missing*

Method — Think about how you would speak it

Read the passage through <u>once</u> before you start <u>correcting the mistakes</u>.
Then read it <u>again</u> really <u>slowly</u>, thinking about where you'd need <u>natural pauses</u>
if you were saying the passage out loud (try to get used to doing this <u>in your head</u>).

1) Write down the <u>first sentence</u> — you need to work out <u>where it ends</u>.

> Charlotte was furious with Ronald her next door neighbour. He kept

This needs a full stop in order for the passage to make sense.

You could add a colon instead of a full stop, because the next bit explains why Charlotte was furious.

2) Now you've <u>created</u> a sentence, think about whether it needs <u>anything else</u>.

These sound like two separate bits, so you need to split them up.

> Charlotte was furious with Ronald   (her next-door neighbour).

There might be more than one way to add punctuation to a sentence.

Brackets split up the sentence nicely, but you could also use a comma.

> Charlotte was furious with Ronald, her next-door neighbour.

For more on when to use brackets, see p.24.

<u>Tips and Tricks for Taking the Test</u>

Don't lose easy marks by forgetting how to start and end sentences correctly.

Plurals

Plural means 'more than one'. So here's a plural number of pages about plurals. Enjoy...

Add 's' to make **Most Words** plural

Most plurals are formed by adding an 's':

Other words have **Different Rules**

Words that **End in 'ch', 'sh', 's', 'x'** and **'z'**

1) Put 'es' at the end of words ending in these letters.
2) You need to add the 'es' to make sure that you keep the soft sound in the original word.

Words that **End in 'o'**

1) Words that end in 'o' usually need 's' to make their plural, e.g. pianos, discos.
2) Some of these words are different though — they take 'es' instead. For example:

| potatoes | tomatoes | heroes | echoes | dominoes |

Words that **End in 'f'** and **'fe'**

1) You need to add 'ves' to many words that end in 'f' and 'fe' to make them plural.

| loaf ⟹ loaves | shelf ⟹ shelves | wife ⟹ wives |

2) But again, some are different. These words just need an 's':

| chiefs | chefs | beliefs | reefs | cliffs | riffs |

Words that **End in 'y'**

1) If the letter before the 'y' is a vowel, just add 's' to make the plural:

toy ⟹ toys

2) If the letter before the 'y' is a consonant, the 'y' becomes 'ies' for the plural:

daisy ⟹ daisies

> Vowels are the letters 'a', 'e', 'i', 'o' and 'u'. All the other letters of the alphabet are consonants.

Irregular Plurals

These words all change their vowel sound when they become plural:

| tooth ⟹ teeth | woman ⟹ women | mouse ⟹ mice |
| man ⟹ men | goose ⟹ geese | oasis ⟹ oases |

You may be asked to **Choose** the **Correct Plural**

> **Q** Circle the correct plural to complete each sentence below.
>
> a) My family owns three *stereoes / stereoss / stereos / steroes*.
> b) The clown at the circus was juggling with *knifes / kniffs / knifies / knives*.
> c) My sister still believes in *faires / fairies / fairys / faireys*.
> d) We have *mouses / mice / mise / mousies* living under the floorboards.

Method — Follow the rules for making plurals

1) Follow the <u>rules</u> to work out the <u>plurals</u>.
2) Remember to look out for any <u>exceptions</u> to the rules (see the previous page).

a) My family owns three *stereoes / stereoss /* (*stereos*) */ steroes*.

The word 'stereo' ends in 'o', so the plural ending has to be 's' or 'es'. ⇒ 'Stereo' takes the 's' ending — so the correct plural is 'stereos'.

b) The clown at the circus was juggling with *knifes / kniffs / knifies /* (*knives*)

'Knife' has an 'fe' ending. Many words ending in 'fe' take the plural 'ves', but some end in 's'. ⇒ The plural of 'knife' takes the more common 'ves' ending, so the answer is 'knives'.

c) My sister still believes in *faires /* (*fairies*) */ fairys / faireys*.

'Fairy' ends with a 'y', so you need to look at the letter before the 'y' to work out the correct plural ending. ⇒ The letter before the 'y' is a consonant — 'r'. So the plural of 'fairy' is 'fairies'.

d) We have *mouses /* (*mice*) */ mise / mousies* living under the floorboards.

The vowel sound of 'mouse' changes when it becomes plural. ⇒ The correct plural form of 'mouse' is 'mice'.

Tips and Tricks for Finding Plurals

You might have to identify misspelt plurals in the test — make sure you follow the rules for forming plurals, but remember the exceptions.

Practice Questions

1) Fill in the gap in each sentence, using the correct plural form of the word in brackets.

a) We watched the monkey swing from the .... (*branch*) of the tree.
b) I always brush my .... (*tooth*) twice a day.
c) We're spending Christmas with the .... (*Grady*). ⬅ *This one is asking for the plural of a name.*
d) Sandy is in the field picking .... (*daisy*).
e) Would you like to try on any of those .... (*dress*)?

Homophones and Homographs

Don't be put off by these complicated words — you probably know loads of homophones already.

Warm-Up Activity

For each of the words below, write down another word that sounds exactly the same, but is spelt differently.

<u>piece</u>   <u>waist</u>   <u>or</u>   <u>sale</u>   <u>sight</u>   <u>male</u>

Homophones *sound the* **Same**

1) Homophones are words that <u>sound the same</u>, but mean <u>different</u> things.

2) Here are lots of examples:

<u>bean</u> and <u>been</u>	<u>root</u> and <u>route</u>	<u>weather</u> and <u>whether</u>
<u>pair</u> and <u>pear</u>	<u>rap</u> and <u>wrap</u>	<u>there</u>, <u>their</u> and <u>they're</u>
<u>wait</u> and <u>weight</u>	<u>blue</u> and <u>blew</u>	<u>by</u>, <u>buy</u> and <u>bye</u>
<u>maid</u> and <u>made</u>	<u>hire</u> and <u>higher</u>	<u>allowed</u> and <u>aloud</u>

Homographs *have the* **Same Spelling**

Homographs don't always sound the same.

1) Homographs are words that have the <u>same spelling</u> but a <u>different meaning</u>.

2) Here is an example:

You need a bow and arrow to be an archer.	Remember to bow to the queen.

The word 'bow' has two different meanings in these sentences.
You only know which meaning it is by reading the rest of the sentence.

A *Pun* is a *Play on Words*

Jokes that use <u>homophones</u> are called <u>puns</u>.

What do rabbits use to comb their fur? A hare brush.

Here 'hare' (an animal like a rabbit) is used instead of 'hair'. The two words are homophones.

I'm on a seafood diet — I see food and I eat it.

Seafood includes things like fish and prawns.

'See food' and 'seafood' are homophones.

You may be asked to **Select** the **Correct Homophone**

> **Q** Circle the correct homophone to complete each sentence below.
>
> a) The supermarket is down by the *quay / key*.
> b) My dog has lovely long *fir / fur*.
> c) My arm was feeling very *saw / sore* when I woke up this morning.
> d) I can't *bear / bare* another day at school today.

Method — Look closely at the spelling of the homophones

1) Work out the <u>meaning</u> of the homophones in each sentence.
2) Then choose the <u>correct</u> homophone to <u>fit</u> the meaning of the sentence.

a) The supermarket is down by the ⟨*quay*⟩ */ key*.

A 'quay' is an area along a waterfront. It's somewhere that you may find a supermarket.

You open a lock using a 'key'. This meaning doesn't fit the sentence.

b) My dog has lovely long *fir /* ⟨*fur*⟩

'fir' is a type of tree.

'fur' is the hair on animals. This is the correct homophone for the sentence.

c) My arm was feeling very *saw /* ⟨*sore*⟩ when I woke up this morning.

'saw' could be the past tense of 'see', or a tool used for cutting wood.

'sore' means 'sensitive' and 'painful'. This is the correct answer — it fits in the sentence.

d) I can't ⟨*bear*⟩ */ bare* another day at school today.

'bear' is an animal, but it also means 'to endure' — this meaning fits the sentence.

'bare' means 'naked' or 'sparse'.

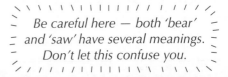

Be careful here — both 'bear' and 'saw' have several meanings. Don't let this confuse you.

Practice Questions

1) Circle the homophones that have been used incorrectly in the passage below.

I'm supposed to go to drama group every Monday knight, but this weak I'm too tired. I've had a very busy day at school and I'm not feeling grate. Instead, I think I'm going to stay hear and watch a film that I haven't scene before.

2) Circle the correct homophone to complete each sentence below.
   a) Make sure that you know *wear / where* you are going.
   b) Watch out for the crab — it has very sharp *claws / clause*.
   c) At the theme park, we *road / rode* on four different roller coasters.
   d) The jockey pulled on the *reigns / reins* to get the horse to stop.

Prefixes and Suffixes

Don't get your fixes in a twist — learn how to use prefixes and suffixes for the test...

Warm-Up Activity

Match the prefixes and suffixes to the correct words.
One has been done for you — 're' and 'match' make 'rematch'.

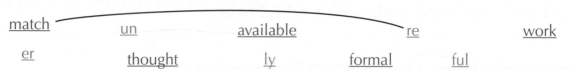

match   un   available   re   work

er   thought   ly   formal   ful

Prefixes go at the Start of Words

Remember — 'pre' = 'before', so prefixes always go at the start of words.

1) Add a prefix at the <u>start</u> of a word to make a <u>new word</u>.

ground ⟹ underground

The word that you add the prefix to is called the <u>root word</u>.

'under' is the prefix

clockwise ⟹ anticlockwise

'anti' is the prefix

2) Here are some <u>common prefixes</u> and an example of a word that uses each one:

ex ⟹ exchange	mis ⟹ misbehave	sub ⟹ submarine
re ⟹ replay	non ⟹ nonsense	inter ⟹ interchange
de ⟹ defrost	pre ⟹ preheat	trans ⟹ transport
un ⟹ unhappy	dis ⟹ disadvantage	counter ⟹ counteract

Suffixes go at the End of Words

1) Add a suffix to the <u>end</u> of a word to make a <u>new word</u>.

garden ⟹ gardener

'garden' is the root word.   'er' is the suffix

turn ⟹ turning

'ing' is the suffix

2) Here's a list of <u>common suffixes</u> with a <u>word</u> that uses each one:

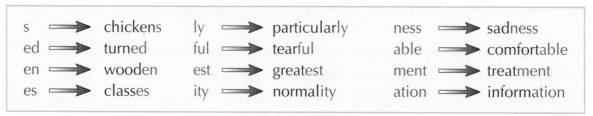

s ⟹ chickens	ly ⟹ particularly	ness ⟹ sadness
ed ⟹ turned	ful ⟹ tearful	able ⟹ comfortable
en ⟹ wooden	est ⟹ greatest	ment ⟹ treatment
es ⟹ classes	ity ⟹ normality	ation ⟹ information

3) Sometimes adding a suffix can <u>change the spelling</u> of the word:

travel ⟹ traveller   stop ⟹ stopping   take ⟹ taking

You could be asked to write the **Correct Prefix** or **Suffix**

Q Write the correct prefix or suffix to complete the words in the sentences.

a) *I asked the waiter for a ...r.....fill of my soft drink.*
b) *It was ....fortunate that you missed the last train home.*
c) *The travell......... left the airport an hour late after their flight was delayed.*
d) *Angus is the tall......... boy in school.*

Method — Read through each sentence carefully

1) You need to add a <u>prefix</u> to parts a) and b). Make sure that
the prefix <u>agrees</u> with the meaning of the <u>rest</u> of the sentence.

> a) I asked the waiter for a refill of my soft drink.

The speaker is asking for another drink.
The word is 'refill', so the correct prefix is 're'.

> b) It was unfortunate that you missed the last train home.

The sentence is talking about having bad luck,
so the correct prefix to add is 'un' to make 'unfortunate'.

2) Look at the <u>whole sentence</u> in parts c) and d) to help you choose the correct <u>suffix</u>.

> c) The travellers left the airport an hour late after their flight was delayed.

You need to add a plural suffix here as the sentence talks
about a group of people. Add 'ers' to make 'travellers'.

'their' tells you that it was
more than one person.

> d) Angus is the tallest boy in school.

You need to add 'est' to make
'tall' into a superlative.

Tips and Tricks for Spelling Questions

If you come across a word with a prefix or a suffix in the test, make sure
it's formed correctly — they like to catch you out with tricky misspellings.

Practice Questions

1) Complete the sentences by adding the correct prefix or suffix to the word in brackets.

a) The baby polar bear is so _____ (*adore*).
b) I was trying to be _____ (*help*) when I washed the dishes.
c) The ball hit Kayley and knocked her _____ (*conscious*).
d) Lyla's feeling of _____ (*happy*) increased when she found her shoes.
e) The apple was covered in mould and the flesh was _____ (*rot*).

The spelling of the root word may change.

Silent Letters and Double Letters

Silent and double letters — making spelling double the fun since 1476...

Warm-Up Activity

A consonant is any letter of the alphabet other than 'a', 'e', 'i', 'o' or 'u'.

Circle the silent <u>consonants</u> in each word.

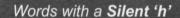

knife   scene   gnome

island   while   lamb   rhyme

Some words have **Silent Letters**

1) Some words are not spelt the way they <u>sound</u>. They have <u>silent letters</u> which you don't hear.

2) Here are some <u>common examples</u>:

Words with a **Silent 'h'**

which	whistle	when
choir	chemist	rhino

Words with a **Silent 'k'**

knock	knife	knuckle
knight	know	knowledge

Lots more words have silent letters — these are some of the common ones.

Words with a **Silent 'b'**

comb	numb	debt
tomb	thumb	doubt

Words with a **Silent 'c'**

yacht	science	scissors
scent	rescind	descend

Words with a **Silent 'w'**

write	wrist	wrong
wrap	answer	who

Words with a **Silent 't'**

listen	whistle
thistle	castle

Words with a **Silent 'l'**

salmon	could
would	should

Words with **Double Letters** can be **Tricky**

Try to think of ways to remember these spellings, e.g. 'necessary' could be 'Never Eat Chips; Eat Salad Sandwiches And Remain Young'.

These words have <u>double letters</u> that you say as a <u>single sound</u>:

accommodation	different	exaggerate	occasion
address	disappear	immediately	occurrence
appalling	embarrass	irresistible	possess
association	essential	jewellery	succeed
deterrent	eventually	necessary	success

Section Three — Spelling

You may have to find **Words** that are **Spelt Wrong**

Q Circle the spelling mistakes in the passage below.

1 ~~Tomorow~~ morning I leave for an ~~autum~~ trip with my youth group. We ~~woud~~
2 like to go to the Lake District as we usually do, but instead we're going to the
3 New Forest. We've got lots of fun ~~acttivities~~ planned like hiking and ~~climing~~,
4 and every ~~knight~~ we will sit by the campfire and eat toasted marshmallows.

Method — Look for silent letters and double letters

1) Work through the passage <u>one line</u> at a time.

2) Look carefully for words that are <u>missing</u> a silent letter,
   or where double letters are used <u>incorrectly</u> or <u>missing</u>.

Tomorrow morning I leave for an autumn trip with my youth group. We would

'Tomorrow' has a double 'r'.   'autumn' has a silent 'n' at the end.   'would' has a silent 'l'.

like to go to the Lake District as we usually do, but instead we're going to the

There are no spelling mistakes in this line.

New Forest. We've got lots of fun activities planned like hiking and climbing.

A double 't' is not needed after 'c'.   'climbing' has a silent 'b'.
It should be spelt as 'activities'.

and every night we will sit by the campfire and eat toasted marshmallows.

This should be 'night' in this context — it isn't spelt
with a silent 'k' when it means the opposite of day.

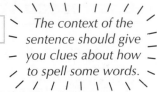
The context of the sentence should give you clues about how to spell some words.

Practice Questions

1) Each sentence below contains one spelling mistake.
   Rewrite the sentences, using the correct word.
   a) *I maintainned a comfortable position for the whole journey.*
   b) *You need to wear more cloths in winter to keep warm.*
   c) *My interresting entry will win the competition tomorrow.*

2) Rewrite the sentences, using the correct word.
   a) Everyone agreed that the charity event had been *successful / successfull / sucessful*.
   b) While we're in London, we want to visit Nelson's *Colum / Collumn / Column*.
   c) Sasha is the most *intelligent / inteligent / inteliggent* girl in the class.
   d) I arrived just as the show was *begining / beginning / beggining*.

Other Awkward Spellings

Bad news, I'm afraid — there are even more words that don't follow the rules.

The 'i' before 'e' rule

1) Learn this rule — it's <u>important</u>:

The whole word doesn't need to rhyme with bee, just the 'ie' sound.

> 'i' before 'e' except after 'c', but only when it rhymes with bee.

2) Here are some examples:

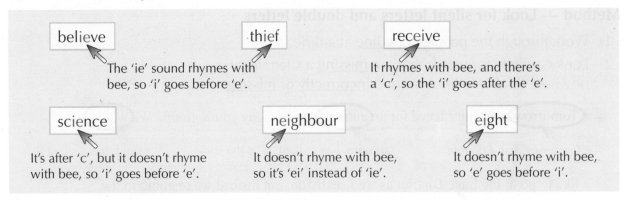

believe
The 'ie' sound rhymes with bee, so 'i' goes before 'e'.

thief

receive
It rhymes with bee, and there's a 'c', so the 'i' goes after the 'e'.

science
It's after 'c', but it doesn't rhyme with bee, so 'i' goes before 'e'.

neighbour
It doesn't rhyme with bee, so it's 'ei' instead of 'ie'.

eight
It doesn't rhyme with bee, so 'e' goes before 'i'.

3) There are a <u>few exceptions</u> to the rule, like '<u>weird</u>' and '<u>seize</u>'.

Unstressed Vowels can make words tricky to spell

1) Sometimes the <u>vowel sound</u> in a word isn't <u>clear</u> — these sounds are called <u>unstressed vowels</u>.

2) Spelling these words can be <u>awkward</u> because the vowels don't make the sound you would <u>expect</u>.

*Make up some short phrases to help you remember how to spell words with unstressed vowels, e.g. "I'm **at** a priv**at**e party".*

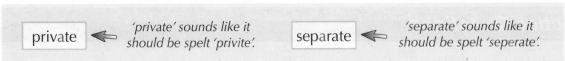

private ← *'private' sounds like it should be spelt 'privite'.*

separate ← *'separate' sounds like it should be spelt 'seperate'.*

3) Unfortunately there isn't a rule for spelling words with <u>unstressed vowels</u> — you'll just have to <u>learn</u> how to spell them. Here are some examples:

definitely	doctor	occurrence
ridiculous	difference	company
government	animal	interference
general	biscuit	carpet
describe	jewellery	miserable

The exam may ask you to **Add Letters** to a **Word**

> **Q** Choose either 'ie' or 'ei' to add to the sentences below.
>
> a) *Adam was rel___ved to find his maths homework.*
> b) *There are p___ces of broken glass everywhere.*
> c) *The villain was very dec___tful.*
> d) *I often w___gh my cat to make sure that she is healthy.*

Method — Remember the 'i before e' rule

1) Work out the <u>word</u> that is being <u>added</u> to each sentence.
2) Think carefully about the spelling — look at the letters <u>before</u> and <u>after</u> the gap.

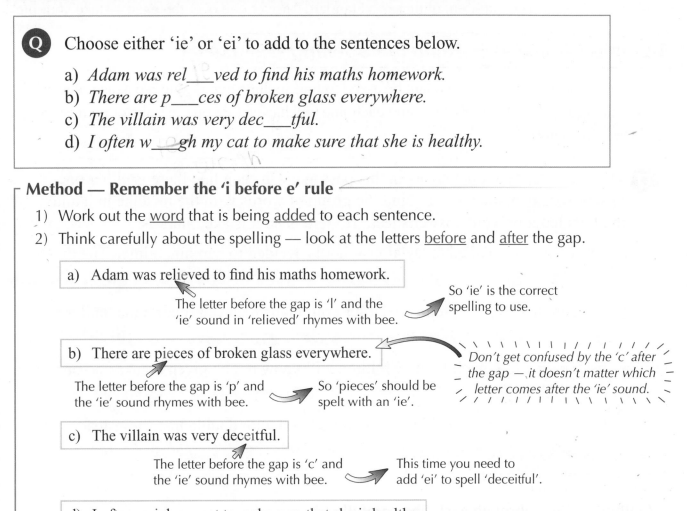

Practice Questions

1) Rewrite the sentences, using the correctly spelt word.

a) My car is running out of *diesel / deisel*.
b) Don't forget to paint the *cieling / ceiling*.
c) Penny's *hieght / height* has increased by 9 cm this year.
d) Mr Harris went to the museum to see the *ancient / anceint* remains.

2) The words below are missing unstressed vowels. Write the correct vowel in each gap.

a) desp__rate
b) fact__ry
c) respons__ble
d) harm__ny
e) lit__r__ture
f) pass__ge

Answering Spelling Questions

Here's a Multiple Choice question, or there's a Standard Answer one over the page — take your pick.

Multiple Choice — Finding the Spelling Mistakes

1) In a <u>Multiple Choice</u> test, you might be asked to find <u>spelling mistakes</u> in a <u>passage</u> of text.

2) The passage will be split into <u>lines</u> and each line will have either <u>one mistake</u> or <u>no mistakes</u>.

3) Here's an example:

> **Q** There are some spelling errors in this passage. On each line there is either one mistake or no mistake at all. Find the group of words with the mistake in it and mark its letter on your answer sheet. If there is no mistake, mark N.
>
> 1   Children were apalled today after schools decided to ban lunchtime. The drastic
>
>   **A**   **B**   **C**   **D**   **N**
>
> 2   measure has been implemented after politicians recieved reports that children
>
>   **A**   **B**   **C**   **D**   **N**
>
> 3   were eating too much food. Children will know not be given breaks and one
>
>   **A**   **B**   **C**   **D**   **N**
>
> 4   teacher beliefs that lunchtime should be filled with double history instead.
>
>   **A**   **B**   **C**   **D**   **N**

Method — Read through each line carefully

1) You need to pick out the <u>incorrectly</u> spelt words. Look out for <u>plural endings</u>, <u>silent letters</u>, <u>double letters</u> and the '<u>i before e</u>' rule as well as other misspelt words.

2) In the exam, you'd mark the <u>letter</u> for the group of words that includes the mistake on your answer sheet.

> 1 Children were appalled today after schools decided to ban lunchtime. The drastic

'appalled' is spelt with a double 'p'. This is the error in this line, so the answer is B.

> 2 measure has been implemented after politicians received reports that children

The 'ie' sound rhymes with bee, and it directly follows a 'c'. So it should be spelt 'received' and the answer is C.

> 3 were eating too much food. Children will now not be given breaks and one

The word 'now' does not have a silent 'k', so the answer is C.

> 4 teacher believes that lunchtime should be filled with double history instead.

'beliefs' is a plural noun — the correct verb form is 'believes', which means the answer is A.

Standard Answer — Correcting Spelling Mistakes

1) On the <u>Standard Answer</u> paper you may be given a passage containing <u>spelling errors</u>.
2) You'll be asked to <u>rewrite</u> the passage, using the <u>correct</u> spellings. Here's an example:

Q The passage below contains some spelling errors.
Rewrite the passage, correcting the spelling mistakes.

Janet was certain that she had mannaged to grow the largest pumpkin this year. She had bean growing the pumpkin for eleven months and it now wieghed over 50 kilograms. She new that the competition would be fierce though; there were usualy at least 20 entrys. Moreover, Janet had no idea how she was going to transport the pumpkin to the awards cerremony witch was taking place the very next day.

(8 marks)

Method — Read the passage carefully

1) Read through the passage at <u>least twice</u>, underlining words that are spelt <u>incorrectly</u>.
2) Next, write down the spellings that you should use <u>instead</u> beside each incorrect word.
3) <u>Rewrite</u> the passage, replacing the incorrectly spelt words with the <u>correct spellings</u>. Check that the passage <u>makes sense</u> and you haven't changed words that <u>were correct</u>.

> Janet was certain that she had managed to grow the largest pumpkin this year.

There is only one 'n' in 'managed'.

> She had been growing the pumpkin for eleven months and it now weighed over 50

'Bean' and 'been' are homophones. 'been' should be used here.

The 'ie' sound does not rhyme with bee, so it should be spelt 'weighed'.

> kilograms. She knew that the competition would be fierce though; there were usually

The verb 'knew' has a silent 'k' which should be added here.

'usually' has a double 'l'.

> at least 20 entries. Moreover, Janet had no idea how she was going to transport the

The plural of 'entry' is spelt 'entries'.

Remember the rule — if the letter before 'y' is a consonant, add 'ies' for the plural endings.

> pumpkin to the awards ceremony which was taking place the very next day.

'ceremony' is spelt with a single 'r'.

'Witch' and 'which' are homophones. 'which' is the correct version to use here.

Tips and Tricks for Spelling Questions

Some of the mistakes may be quite tricky to spot in the passage, so make sure you really **look** and think about each word. Don't just skim-read the text.

Alliteration and Onomatopoeia

English is full of long words for really simple things — here are two of them...

Alliteration is the repetition of **Consonant Sounds**

1) Alliteration is the repetition of a sound at the beginning of nearby words.

2) It emphasises certain words and makes a sentence more memorable.

> Sally slipped on a slimy slug.

There are lots of 's' and 'sl' sounds in this sentence.

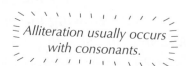

Alliteration usually occurs with consonants.

> The dirty dog drooled all over the doormat.

In this sentence, the 'd' sound is repeated.

Onomatopoeia is when a word **Sounds** *like the* **Noise** *it* **Describes**

1) Onomatopoeic words sound like the noise they describe.

2) Here are some examples:

| fizz | bang | crash | crunch | splash | plop | drip |

You may be asked to identify **Onomatopoeic** *words in a* **Passage**

Q Circle the onomatopoeic words in the passage below.

Amy signalled to Joe and they sneaked into the garage. The ladder scraped across the floor as they tried to move it. They carried the ladder and put it up against the tree. As soon as they did, Tiddles miaowed happily and pattered safely down.

Method — Look for words that describe noises

1) Read through the passage looking for words that sound like the noise they're describing.

2) If you're not sure about a word, say it to yourself. Listen carefully to the sound it makes.

> Amy signalled to Joe and they sneaked into the garage. The ladder scraped across

These words aren't onomatopoeic — they don't sound like a noise.

'scraped' is onomatopoeic — it sounds like the noise it is describing.

> the floor as they tried to move it. They carried the ladder and put it up against

There are no onomatopoeic words in this line.

> the tree. As soon as they did, Tiddles miaowed happily and pattered safely down.

'miaowed' sounds like the noise a cat makes — this is onomatopoeic.

'pattered' is also onomatopoeic.

Make sure that you can spot **Alliteration** in a **Sentence**

Q Circle the letters that alliterate in these sentences.

a) *Michael's scary school project scooped first prize.*

b) *The king kept kicking the kind knight.*

c) *She surely made the sugar shapes.*

d) *Felicity photographed forests for her family.*

Method — Find the sound that's repeated in the sentence

1) You have to <u>circle</u> the <u>sounds</u> that are <u>repeated</u>.

2) Listen to the <u>sound</u> made by the letters at the <u>beginning</u> of each word in the sentence.

Remember that alliteration is the repetition of the same sound rather than the same letter.

a) Michael's (scary (school project (scooped first prize.

The 'sc' sound alliterates in this sentence.

b) The (king (kept (kicking the (kind knight.

This sentence has a repeated 'k' sound. Although 'knight' begins with a 'k', this letter is silent so it doesn't alliterate with the other words. The 'k' in the middle of 'kicking' doesn't alliterate because it's in the middle of the word.

c) (She (surely made the (sugar (shapes.

The 'sh' sound alliterates in this sentence. You need to circle the 'su' of 'surely' and 'sugar' too — although they are spelt with 'su' they begin with an 'sh' sound.

Saying the sentence in your head will help you to hear the sounds each word makes.

d) (Felicity (photographed (forests (for her (family.

In this sentence it's the 'f' sound that is repeated — even though 'photographed' is spelt with a 'ph', it's still pronounced with an 'f'.

Practice Questions

1) Say whether each sentence is an example of onomatopoeia, alliteration or neither.

a) *Carol circled the church.*

b) *The door banged in the wind.*

c) *Studying psychology suits Susan.*

d) *He shouted loudly as the train sped past.*

e) *Whose work is wrong?*

f) *The chickens clucked in the yard.*

Imagery

Imagery is another word for descriptive writing — it's often used in fiction texts.

Figurative Language gives you a *Picture*

1) <u>Literal language</u> means <u>exactly</u> what it says.

> Dave is a real clown. ← If you are talking about someone called Dave who works as a clown, then this is a literal statement.

2) <u>Figurative language</u> doesn't mean exactly what it says.

> Dave is a real clown. ← If you're describing someone who jokes around a lot but who isn't actually a clown, then this is a figurative statement.

3) <u>Imagery</u> is a type of <u>figurative language</u> — it's <u>language</u> that is used to give the reader a <u>vivid picture</u> of something.

> The field of tulips I saw from the window was like a red carpet stretching into the distance.

This imagery makes you imagine a red carpet in your mind, and this shows you what the field of tulips was like.

> The pie smelt like rotten egg, and its crust was concrete.

This imagery helps you to imagine what the pie smelt like...

... and this imagery tells you how hard the crust was, but you know it isn't actually made of concrete.

There are lots of different types of *Imagery*

A *Simile* says that *One Thing* is *Like Another*

1) A <u>simile</u> describes something by <u>comparing it</u> to something else.
2) Similes always use a <u>comparing word</u> like '<u>as</u>' or '<u>like</u>'.

> His anger erupted like a volcano.

The simile helps you to imagine the force of his anger.

> Jackie's cheeks were as white as snow.

This simile emphasises how white Jackie's cheeks were.

> Life is like a rollercoaster.

Life is being compared to a rollercoaster in this simile.

A *Metaphor* says that *One Thing Is Another*

1) A <u>metaphor</u> describes something as <u>actually being</u> something else.
2) It's an example of <u>figurative writing</u>.

> Jack's eyes were deep black oily pools.

This gives a vivid description of Jack's eyes, but they're not actually deep black oily pools.

> The living room was a furnace.

The living room wasn't actually a furnace, but the metaphor shows that the room was very hot.

Tips and Tricks for Imagery Questions

The difference between similes and metaphors can be pretty confusing. Remember, if a sentence <u>compares</u> something to something else, then it's a simile. If it says that something <u>is</u> something else, then it's a metaphor.

Analogies are like *Extended Similes*

1) An <u>analogy</u> is a <u>comparison</u> between two similar things.
2) It <u>compares</u> two different things to help <u>explain</u> something to the reader.

> The rainforest is being cut down at an incredible speed. An area of rainforest equal to twenty football pitches is lost every minute.

This part is the analogy. It helps you to visualise exactly how quickly the rainforest is being cut down.

Personification describes a *Thing* as a *Person*

Personification makes descriptions come to life.

<u>Personification</u> describes something that's not human as if it is a <u>person</u>.

> The sea races up the beach.

This sounds like the sea has the ability to run.

> The sun smiled on the shoppers below.

This sounds like the sun has a human expression.

> Time had been kind to Raj; there was not a wrinkle on his face.

This sounds like time was deliberately nice to Raj.

Section Four — Word Types

You may have to **Recognise Different Types of Imagery**

Q Read the passage below. Then answer the questions that follow.

It was the hottest day of summer. The sun was a golden lamp in the sky, casting rays onto the sunbathers who were lying on the sand. Cries of excitement from the seagulls competed for attention with the shouts of ice cream sellers strolling along the beach. Like a swan crossing a lake, a boat cruised slowly past in the distance.

a) Find one example of a simile in the passage.
b) Give one example of personification in the passage.
c) Give one example of a metaphor from the passage.

Method — Look closely for different types of imagery

1) Read through the <u>whole passage</u>. Start to look for the <u>different types</u> of imagery.

2) For <u>part a)</u> you need to find a <u>simile</u>. Look for comparisons using 'like' or 'as ... as'.

Like a swan crossing a lake, a boat cruised slowly past in the distance.

The boat in the distance is compared to a swan crossing a lake. This is a simile.

3) <u>Part b)</u> asks you to find an example of <u>personification</u>. You need to find a point in the passage where something is given <u>human qualities</u>.

Cries of excitement from the seagulls competed for attention

Saying that the seagulls cried out with "excitement" gives them a human quality, so it's an example of personification.

4) You need to find a <u>metaphor</u> for <u>part c)</u>. Look for a place where something is <u>described as</u> something else.

You could use imagery like similes and metaphors in your writing to make it more interesting — have a look at p. 75 for more.

The sun was a golden lamp in the sky,

The sun is described as being 'a golden lamp' — this is a metaphor.

Practice Questions

1) Write down whether each sentence is a simile, a metaphor, or personification.

a) *Luck had not been kind to Karl — his trousers had ripped in two.*
b) *Fatima's clothes were as heavy as a coat of armour.*
c) *The cold hand of fear gripped Luke's heart.*
d) *The packed classroom was as silent as a library.*
e) *Gary's fingers were icicles when he'd finished playing volleyball in the snow.*

Abbreviations

You see acronyms and initialisms everywhere. Make sure you know the difference between them.

Warm-Up Activity

Match the abbreviations in blue below to their full spelling in red.

 Dr   United Kingdom   ttyl   Doctor   Jan

                sci-fi   January   UK

science fiction
                Football Club   FC   talk to you later

Abbreviations *are* **Shortened Words**

You might see abbreviations in books or newspapers. If you don't know what they stand for, try to find out.

1) Abbreviations are shortened versions of words, for example:

| bicycle | ⟹ | bike | | refrigerator | ⟹ | fridge | | hippopotamus | ⟹ | hippo |

2) Longer phrases can be shortened in two main ways:

Initialisms *are Said as* **Letters**

Initialisms use the first letters of words in a phrase — they are pronounced as separate letters.

| PC = personal computer | | UN = United Nations | | PTO = please turn over |

Acronyms *are Said as* **Words**

Acronyms usually use the first letters of words in a phrase to make a new word.

| NATO = North Atlantic Treaty Organisation |

Sometimes more than one letter from each word is used to form the acronym.

| Radar = radio detection and ranging | ⟸ The 'ra' at the start of radio make up the first two letters of 'radar'.

Practice Questions

1) Give the abbreviated version of each of these words.
   a) rhinoceros   b) electronic mail   c) influenza

2) Give the full word for these abbreviations.
   a) dino   b) telly   c) lab

3) Write down whether each word below is an abbreviation, an initialism or an acronym.
   a) CD   b) approx.   c) NASA   d) DVD   e) BBC

Irony and Rhetorical Questions

Which metal is the most sarcastic? Iron-y.

Warm-Up Activity

1) Find an <u>old</u> newspaper or magazine that nobody is using.
2) Read the adverts, and try to find <u>5 examples</u> of <u>questions</u>.
3) See if you can find any questions where the answer is <u>not given</u> in the <u>advert</u>.

Irony is often used to **Create Humour**

Verbal Irony is where the ***Opposite Meaning*** *is meant*

There's more about literal meaning on page 48.

1) <u>Verbal irony</u> is where the writer means the <u>opposite</u> to what they have <u>actually written</u>.
2) You can usually tell that the writer is being ironic from the <u>context</u> of the writing.

> We were stranded at the airport for 48 hours with no food, which was just great.

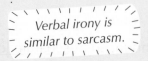

Verbal irony is similar to sarcasm.

The writer doesn't actually mean that it was great — they actually mean the opposite. This is irony.

Situational Irony is where ***Unexpected Events Occur***

<u>Situational irony</u> is where the <u>opposite</u> thing happens to what the reader <u>expects</u>.

> While the two robbers were robbing the bank, someone stole their car.

We don't expect someone to steal from the robbers. This is an example of situational irony — it is the opposite of what we expect to happen.

A **Rhetorical Question Isn't** *a* **Proper Question**

1) A <u>rhetorical question</u> is a question that you are <u>not expected</u> to answer.
2) They are often designed to make you <u>think</u>, or to make you <u>do something</u>.

> When will the world take notice of what is going on?

Rhetorical questions are often used in newspapers or adverts.

This a rhetorical question — no one knows the answer. It is designed to make you think about what is happening.

> How many times have I told you not to run in the corridor?

You're not meant to answer this question. The speaker is reminding you that you should not run in the corridor.

You may be asked to spot **Irony** and **Rhetorical Questions**

Q Read the passage below. Then answer the questions that follow.

"Have you ever heard such a ridiculous excuse?" asked Mrs Henningway when Mildred told her that her homework had blown away. "It's even worse because you forgot your homework last week as well, didn't you?" Mildred admitted that she had indeed forgotten her homework the previous week, but this hadn't been her fault either, as her computer had broken. "Of course, none of this matters," continued Mrs Henningway. "It's not as if doing your homework will help you to pass your exams."

a) Find one example of irony in the passage.

b) Give one example of a rhetorical question in the passage.

Method — Look for irony and unanswered questions

1) You need to find an example of <u>irony</u> in the passage for part a). Remember that this can be found when someone is <u>speaking</u>.

> "It's not as if doing your homework will help you to pass your exams."

This is verbal irony — Mrs Henningway means the opposite. Doing her homework will help Mildred to pass her exams.

2) For part b) you need to find a <u>rhetorical question</u> — look for an <u>unanswered question</u> in the passage.

Mildred answers the other question that Mrs Henningway asks her — she admits that she had forgotten her homework the week before.

> "Have you ever heard such a ridiculous excuse?"

This is a rhetorical question. You can tell this because Mrs Henningway doesn't expect Mildred to answer it, and so she continues to speak.

Practice Questions

1) Read the following sentences. Put a tick next to the ones that show irony.

a) *I play hockey on Saturdays whether it rains or not.*

b) *Ed had saved up all year for his new toy, only to be given it for Christmas.*

c) *I went to the shop to buy gravy granules and they were on special offer.*

d) *Maggie stepped around a puddle and ended up falling into a pond.*

e) *I'm allergic to apples, but my brother is allergic to pears.*

Idioms, Clichés and Proverbs

Idioms, clichés and proverbs are different types of phrases — you hear them all the time.

Warm-Up Activity

1) Look at the <u>common phrases</u> below.
2) For each phrase, try to write <u>one of your own</u> that means <u>exactly</u> the same thing.

Every cloud has a silver lining.   The early bird catches the worm.

That was a piece of cake.   It's raining cats and dogs outside.

Idioms are Phrases that Aren't Meant Literally

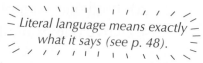

Literal language means exactly what it says (see p. 48).

1) <u>Idioms</u> are <u>common phrases</u> that most people use and understand.
2) They have a meaning that is <u>different</u> to the <u>literal meaning</u> of the words.
3) You can only understand an idiom if you <u>know</u> what it means.

Break a leg ← Literally, this means that you're telling someone to break a bone, but it's also an idiom used to wish actors luck before a performance.

Under the weather ← This idiom is used to describe people who are feeling ill.

Keep your hair on ← This idiom is used to tell someone to calm down.

Clichés are Overused Phrases

Try not to use clichés in your writing — they're really unoriginal.

1) A <u>cliché</u> is a phrase that has been <u>overused</u> and has <u>lost</u> some of its <u>impact</u>.
2) Clichés are often <u>metaphors</u> (see page 49).

I gave 110%. ← Some people use this cliché to show how much effort they put into something. It doesn't really mean anything though — you can't give more than 100% effort.

Avoid it like the plague. ← This is another common cliché. It basically means that something is really unappealing.

3) Many <u>idioms</u> are also <u>clichés</u> because they're <u>common phrases</u> that people use a lot.

Proverbs are Phrases that Give Advice

1) <u>Proverbs</u> are <u>short phrases</u> that are commonly used.
2) They usually give a <u>general truth</u> or <u>words of advice</u> for how to do something.

Too many cooks spoil the broth.

This means that it's a bad idea to have too many people doing the same thing.

Don't judge a book by its cover.

This proverb means that you shouldn't judge people or objects by the way they look.

Make sure that you can recognise **Idioms**, **Clichés** and **Proverbs**

Q Each sentence below contains either an idiom or a proverb.
Write down which type is used in each sentence.

a) *My brother is really winding me up today.*
b) *Ben's got a chip on his shoulder.*
c) *Look after the pennies and the pounds will look after themselves.*

Method — Think about each sentence's meaning

Identify the <u>phrase</u> in each sentence and think
about whether it's an <u>idiom</u> or a <u>proverb</u>.

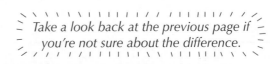
*Take a look back at the previous page if
you're not sure about the difference.*

a) My brother is really winding me up today.

'winding me up' is a common phrase. The person isn't actually being
wound up though — it means that they're being annoyed. This is an idiom.

b) Ben's got a chip on his shoulder.

This sentence means Ben's angry about something — he doesn't literally have
a chip on his shoulder. This sentence isn't giving advice, so it's an idiom.

c) Look after the pennies and the pounds will look after themselves.

This whole sentence is a proverb — it means that if you
save small amounts, it'll add up to bigger savings.

Tips and Tricks for Identifying Common Phrases

If you need to identify a proverb or idiom in the exam, think about what the phrase is doing.

If it's giving advice, it's a proverb, but if it's more like a common phrase, it's an idiom.

Practice Questions

1) Write out the literal meaning of each of the following:

a) *You're going to end up in hot water if you carry on like this.*
b) *I put blood, sweat and tears into my maths homework.*
c) *It's time to throw in the towel.*
d) *I wish the politician would stop beating about the bush.*
e) *My little brother is really driving me up the wall.*

Synonyms and Antonyms

Just when you thought you'd learnt all the tricky words, here are two more — synonym and antonym

Warm-Up Activity

1) Ask someone else to join you. Each person needs a <u>pen</u> and a <u>piece of paper</u>.
2) For <u>each word</u> below, you both need to think of <u>three words</u> that mean the <u>same</u> and <u>three words</u> that mean the <u>opposite</u>.
3) The winner is the <u>first person</u> to do this <u>correctly</u> for all of the words.

<u>wise</u>   <u>love</u>   <u>brave</u>   <u>fast</u>

Synonyms are words that Mean the Same

> *Using synonyms can improve your writing — they can stop you repeating the same words over again. Have a look at p.74.*

1) Words that can mean the <u>same thing</u> are <u>synonyms</u>.
2) Here are a few examples of synonyms:

| cross | ⟹ | angry, furious, annoyed, irritated, irate |

These are all synonyms for the word 'cross'.

| happy | ⟹ | joyful, merry, content, cheerful, jolly |

| scared | ⟹ | afraid, fearful, agitated, alarmed, worried, frightened |

Antonyms are words that Mean the Opposite

1) <u>Antonyms</u> are words like 'hot' and 'cold' — they are <u>opposites</u>.
2) These are examples of antonyms:

Anti‑

| fun | ⟹ | dull, boring, tedious, tiresome, unexciting |

These are all antonyms of the word 'fun'.

| bad | ⟹ | good, great, amazing, fantastic, brilliant |

> *There's more about prefixes and suffixes on page 38.*

Antonyms can be made by adding a Prefix to a Root Word...

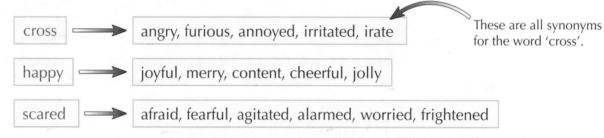

helpful ⟹ unhelpful   appear ⟹ disappear   behave ⟹ misbehave

... or by changing a Suffix

careful ⟹ careless   painful ⟹ painless   tactful ⟹ tactless

Q Read the passage and then answer the questions that follow.

The owl sat upon the bridge feeling disgruntled, staring down at her reflection in the water below. Only that morning she had been the wisest owl in the forest, but that accolade had been taken by her ecstatic sister. Her eyes suddenly focused on the pool below as a small face broke the surface.

1) Pick a word from the passage that means the same as 'annoyed'.

2) Pick a word from the passage that means the opposite of 'miserable'.

Method — Think carefully about what each word means

1) Work out the <u>meaning</u> of the <u>word</u> in the <u>question</u>, then read the text again.
2) If you <u>don't know</u> what the word in the question means, look for <u>clues</u> in the passage.
3) Question 1 asks you to find a word that means the same as '<u>annoyed</u>':

| The owl sat upon the bridge feeling disgruntled... |

'disgruntled' has the same meaning as 'annoyed', so that's the answer.

Look at the passage to help you. The owl is upset because she's no longer the wisest, so you can guess that 'disgruntled' means 'annoyed'.

4) For question 2, you need to find the <u>opposite</u> of '<u>miserable</u>':

| ...but that accolade had been taken by her ecstatic sister. |

'ecstatic' means very happy, so it has the opposite meaning to 'miserable'.

Her sister has just become the wisest owl, so if you're not sure, you can guess that 'ecstatic' means happy.

Practice Questions

1) Circle the correct synonym for the word in bold.
   a) Losing my job left me feeling **desolate** (*hopeless / disappointed / furious*).
   b) The dark clouds overhead were **ominous** (*drifting / threatening / depressing*).
   c) The boy walked to his lesson **briskly** (*indifferently / hurriedly / precisely*).

2) Circle the correct antonym for the word in bold.
   a) Max shouted at her in a **patronising** way (*helpful / respectful / cheeky*).
   b) The news left my grandparents **jubilant** (*overjoyed / concerned / despondent*).
   c) The assembly was very **tedious** (*arduous / stimulating / boring*).

Answering Word Type Questions

There's nothing like a couple of sample questions to help you get ready for the exam...

Multiple Choice — Identifying Word Types

1) In the test, you might be asked questions about the <u>word types</u> a writer has used.

2) You'll be asked to <u>read</u> a passage and then answer some <u>questions</u> about <u>what you've read</u>.

3) Here's an example of the sort of thing you might see in the test:

Q Read the poem below and then answer the following questions.

An extract from *Summer Evening* by John Clare

> 1 *Crows crowd croaking overhead,*
> 2 *Hastening to the woods to bed.*
> 3 *Cooing sits the lonely dove,*
> 4 *Calling home her absent love.*
> 5 *With 'Kirchup! Kirchup!' 'mong the wheats,*
> 6 *Partridge distant partridge greets;*

This is just an extract — the text in the test will usually be longer than this.

1) What is '*Crows crowd croaking overhead*' (line 1) an example of?
   A Rhetorical Question
   B Personification
   C Alliteration
   D A metaphor
   E Irony

2) What is '*Cooing*' (line 3) an example of?
   A Alliteration
   B Personification
   C Onomatopoeia
   D A simile
   E Situational irony

Method — Read the examples in the question carefully

Look at the context of the passage to help you work out the techniques that the author has used.

1) Think about the <u>techniques</u> mentioned in each question. Look at the <u>line reference</u> to find the quote in the poem.

2) Read the <u>quote</u> in question 1. Look for <u>patterns</u> in the <u>word sounds</u> and think about whether the meaning is <u>literal</u> or <u>figurative</u>.

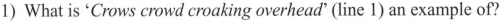

> Crows crowd croaking overhead ← The poet has repeated the 'cr' sound — this is an example of alliteration.

3) You can work out the answer to question 2 by thinking about <u>what the word sounds like</u>.

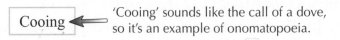

> Cooing ← 'Cooing' sounds like the call of a dove, so it's an example of onomatopoeia.

Look at the remaining options to check that you've chosen the correct technique.

Standard Answer — *Finding Word Types in a passage*

Q Read the passage below and then answer the questions that follow.

Selworth — worth visiting?

1 *Wide sandy beaches. Picturesque vistas. These are just some of the things that you won't witness if you choose to spend your holiday this year in Selworth. Instead, you can expect to hear the constant whine of traffic, the clanging of heavy machinery and the ferocious shouts of the locals going about their daily lives.*

5 *Of course, there is still the famous Selworth Castle. Sadly, the 'insightful and historical day out' offered by the guidebook is not granted by the steep admission prices and the sheer overcrowding. I was like a rush-hour commuter on the Underground trying to move between rooms; I decided to call it a day after 45 minutes and go for a bowl of soup in the restaurant, but it was cold.*

1) The word '*clanging*' (line 3) is an example of which technique?

2) '*I was like a rush-hour commuter on the Underground*' (lines 7-8). Which type of imagery is used here?

3) Find an example of an idiom in the passage.

Method — Think carefully about the different word types

1) Question 1 asks you to name which technique is used in the word '<u>clanging</u>':

> ...the clanging of heavy machinery...   ⟵   The word 'clanging' sounds like the noise it makes. So 'clanging' is an example of onomatopoeia.

2) For question 2, think about the <u>different types</u> of <u>imagery</u>:

> I was like a rush-hour commuter on the Underground   ⟵   The key word is 'like' — the author compares their experience to being a rush-hour commuter. This is an example of a simile.

3) You need to find an example of an <u>idiom</u> in the passage for question 3.
Look for a phrase where the <u>literal</u> meaning is <u>different</u> to the <u>intended</u> meaning.

> ...I decided to call it a day after 45 minutes...   ⟵   The author didn't literally 'call it a day'. Instead, it means that they gave up and did something else. So 'call it a day' is an idiom.

<u>Tips and Tricks for Word Type Questions</u>

If you're taking a Standard Answer test, think about the meaning behind the words and the effect created by the technique to help you identify the technique or word type used.

Section Five —

Sectio

Reading the Text

Comprehension texts come in all shapes and sizes — here's how to tackle them...

Warm-Up Activity

1) Find an unwanted <u>magazine</u> and <u>newspaper</u>.
2) <u>Cut</u> out an <u>article</u> from each of them.
3) For both articles, write down a <u>key word</u> which sums up each paragraph.

Texts can be **Divided** into **Fiction** and **Non-fiction**

1) <u>Fiction</u> texts are <u>made up</u> by the author, and are about <u>imaginary events</u> and <u>people</u>. <u>Non-fiction</u> texts are based on <u>facts</u>, and are about <u>real people</u> and <u>events</u>.

2) Here are some <u>examples</u> of the types of texts you might get in your reading comprehension:

Fiction Texts

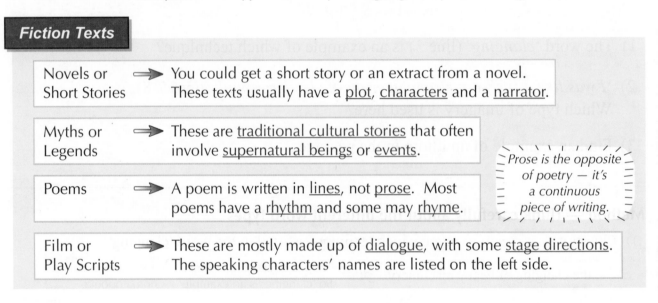

Novels or Short Stories ⟹ You could get a short story or an extract from a novel. These texts usually have a <u>plot</u>, <u>characters</u> and a <u>narrator</u>.

Myths or Legends ⟹ These are <u>traditional cultural stories</u> that often involve <u>supernatural beings</u> or <u>events</u>.

Poems ⟹ A poem is written in <u>lines</u>, not <u>prose</u>. Most poems have a <u>rhythm</u> and some may <u>rhyme</u>.

Prose is the opposite of poetry — it's a continuous piece of writing.

Film or Play Scripts ⟹ These are mostly made up of <u>dialogue</u>, with some <u>stage directions</u>. The speaking characters' names are listed on the left side.

Non-fiction Texts

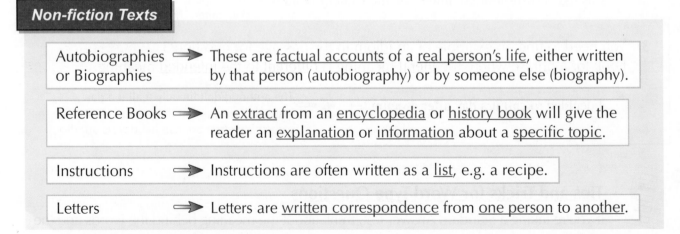

Autobiographies or Biographies ⟹ These are <u>factual accounts</u> of a <u>real person's life</u>, either written by that person (autobiography) or by someone else (biography).

Reference Books ⟹ An <u>extract</u> from an <u>encyclopedia</u> or <u>history book</u> will give the reader an <u>explanation</u> or <u>information</u> about a <u>specific topic</u>.

Instructions ⟹ Instructions are often written as a <u>list</u>, e.g. a recipe.

Letters ⟹ Letters are <u>written correspondence</u> from <u>one person</u> to <u>another</u>.

Comprehension Questions *ask you to* Pick Out Details

You can use this <u>method</u> to tackle <u>comprehension questions</u> in the test.

Make sure that your highlighting doesn't slow down your reading too much.

Method — Highlighting key words saves time

1) As you read, <u>scan</u> the text looking for <u>information</u> which gives you the <u>main points</u> of the text, and <u>highlight</u> a few <u>key words</u>.

2) <u>Key words</u> are things that tell you <u>who</u>, <u>what</u>, <u>where</u>, <u>when</u>, <u>why</u> and <u>how</u>.

This tells you what the passage is about. →

> Not much is known about the origins of Stonehenge. Nobody knows when it was erected, but most historians think that it must have happened between 3000 and 2000 BC. Equally, it is unclear why it was built; some scholars argue that it served a religious purpose, but others think that it was a kind of observatory, to study the movements of the stars and planets.

These dates would be helpful in a 'when' question.

These purposes would be helpful in a 'why question'.

3) Read the <u>questions</u>, using the <u>key words</u> that you've <u>highlighted</u> as <u>signposts</u> to help you find <u>where</u> the <u>important information</u> is in the text.

This question asks 'when', so you need to look for dates.

Q 1) When does the text suggest Stonehenge was built?

2) What reasons does the text give for its construction?

This question asks 'what reasons', so you need to look for purposes.

Practice Questions

1) Read the passage below and then answer the questions that follow.

1 *Joaquin couldn't believe his eyes. Standing in front of him was Eric Debuski,*
2 *lead vocalist of the 'Island Sandmen'. Eric, otherwise known as Lavahead, wasn't*
3 *wearing his trademark deerhunter and aviators, but there was no doubt about it.*
4 *It was him all right! Joaquin had worked here for two whole years and this was the*
5 *most exciting thing that had happened in all that time. He'd never met anyone famous*
6 *before, and now he was meeting the frontman of his favourite band. It was astounding.*
7 *"Hey kid," Eric said commandingly, "you might want to try shutting that mouth."*
8 *Joaquin swallowed loudly. "S-S-Sorry", he stammered, as he scanned through Eric's*
9 *basket. Eric just stood back and gazed lazily, almost as if he were a normal person.*

a) What is Eric Debuski's stage name?

b) What word in the passage can mean the same as 'lead vocalist' (line 2)?

c) What kind of place does Joaquin work in?

d) Why do you think Eric tells Joaquin to shut his mouth?

e) What evidence is there in the passage which suggests how Joaquin was feeling?

Understanding the Questions

Here are some lovely pages about 'Understanding the Questions'— just my cup of tea.

Make sure you *Learn* the *Different Question Types*

1) You need to use <u>different skills</u> for different <u>question types</u>.
2) <u>Learn</u> to recognise question types so you know <u>how</u> to <u>answer</u> them.

The same question types come up in both standard answer and multiple choice tests. See p.64-67 for more about the two question styles.

Fact Recall Questions

Fact recall questions usually use words like <u>who</u>, <u>where</u>, <u>what</u>, <u>when</u>, <u>why</u> and <u>how</u>:

> What are the names of the two brothers?
> When did the ship set sail?

You should be able to find answers to these questions simply by reading through the passage carefully.

Method — Find the facts

1) First, you need to look at the <u>question</u> to find out <u>what</u> you are <u>looking for</u>. You may need to read between the lines if the answer is <u>not obvious</u>.

> Who is George's oldest son?

'Who' tells you that you're looking for a name. 'oldest' tells you to look for information about ages.

2) Scan the text for the <u>information</u> that will help you <u>work out</u> the answer.

Buster is the youngest, so it can't be him.

> George had four sons: Mike, Oscar, Toby and Buster. As the youngest, Buster was spoiled growing up, whilst Mike and Toby competed over who was the favourite middle child.

The oldest must be one of these four.

Mike and Toby are the middle children, so it can't be them.

3) This information shows that <u>Oscar</u> must be the <u>oldest son</u>.

Questions about Word Meanings

You might need to use your knowledge of <u>word meanings</u> to answer a question:

> How did Cody feel about the state of the kitchen?

The key words in the question tell you what it is asking.

Method — Think about word meanings

1) Once you know what the question is <u>asking</u>, you can <u>find</u> the <u>information</u> in the text:

> Cody was repulsed by what he saw in the kitchen.

The text tells you how he feels.

2) If the question gives you options, <u>choose</u> the one that has the <u>closest meaning</u>:

> A He was delighted.
> B He was appalled.
> C He was disgusted.
> D He was confused.
> E He was astounded.

Out of all the options 'disgusted' is the closest to 'repulsed', so C is the answer.

See p.56-57 for more advice on questions about word meaning.

Section Five — Comprehension

Multiple Statement Questions

You may be given a <u>list</u> of <u>statements</u> and asked which ones are <u>right</u> or <u>wrong</u>.
You need to choose a letter from <u>A to E</u> that matches the right <u>combination of options</u>.

Method — Narrow down the options

According to the text who were the last two conservative prime ministers?

1. Margaret Thatcher   2. Tony Blair
3. David Cameron   4. John Major

A   1 and 2
B   2 and 3
C   2 and 4 ⟵ You need to pick out the letter which matches
D   1 and 4   the correct combination of options.
E   3 and 4

Some multiple statement questions just ask for one answer, e.g. 'Which of these statements is true?'

You need to work out which <u>two options</u> are correct, using <u>information</u> from the text.

The Conservative Party dominated British politics during the 1980s and early 1990s. Margaret Thatcher was Prime Minister from 1979 to 1990, followed by John Major from 1990 to 1997. After that, the Labour Party regained power with the election of Tony Blair. They remained in power lead by Gordon Brown until 2010 when the Conservatives won the vote and David Cameron came to office.

Here's one of the answers...

...and here's the other answer. So you need the letter which matches option 3 and 4 — letter E.

Reasoning Questions

Reasoning questions ask about the text's <u>purpose</u> or <u>meaning</u>.

You might need to use common sense to work out the answers to some reasoning questions.

1) These questions could use phrases like '<u>most likely</u>' or ask you about the <u>opinions</u> of the <u>author</u> or <u>characters</u>.

These questions are asking about the passage's ⟹ purpose.

Why does Amir keep his prize a secret?
What is the writer's view of wine in general?
Where would you be most likely to read this passage?

If a question asks you about something that isn't in the text, look for clues in the information you've been given.

2) Questions that ask '<u>why</u>' or '<u>what do you think</u>' might test your own <u>opinion</u>. <u>Think about</u> the <u>impression</u> you get from the text's <u>language</u> and <u>tone</u>.

Questions about Grammar and Literary Techniques

You might get a question about <u>grammar</u> and <u>literary techniques</u>:

What type of word is 'tweeted'?

You should look at the sentence that the word is from to work out the answer.

See Section 1 and Section 4 for detailed advice on how to answer these types of question.

Answering Comprehension Questions

Here are some cracking comprehension questions with advice on how to answer them.

Multiple Choice Questions give you Several Possible Options

1) In <u>Multiple Choice questions</u> the answer is always <u>given</u>. You just need to <u>pick</u> the <u>right one</u>.

2) When the <u>possible options</u> are <u>similar</u>, it can make the question more <u>difficult</u>. The best way to tackle each question is to work through it carefully, <u>step by step</u>.

Q Read the passage below. Then answer the question that follows.

1   *The problem was not that the film was three hours long, or that the acting was*
2   *atrocious, but that the plot was incomprehensible. I have no idea what Captain Jutter*
3   *had to do with anything, partly because I could not understand a word he said, but also*
4   *because he disappeared halfway through the film, without any explanation. I don't*
5   *think it was ever explained exactly why the pirates had to get back to Shadow Island;*
6   *all I know is that it was of "great importance". The screenwriter, Jordan Vidal, needs*
7   *to take a long, hard look in the mirror after this terrible mishap of an adventure film.*

1) According to the passage, what was the film's main downfall?

   A The screenwriter was not very good.
   B The acting was terrible.
   C The story was too complicated.
   D It didn't make any sense.
   E It was too long.

> *Be wary of options that are mentioned in the text but don't answer the question, as they could mislead you. Always double-check that your answer matches the text.*

Method — Find the important information

1) First, look for any <u>key words</u> relating to the question (you may have highlighted them during your first read-through):

'problem' means the same as 'downfall'. →

> The problem was not that the film was three hours long, or that the acting was atrocious, but that the plot was incomprehensible.

← This sentence mentions three possible answers to the question.

The sentence tells you that the problem was not the length of the film or the acting, so it cannot be option B or E.

2) <u>Check</u> this information <u>against the options</u>.

   A The screenwriter was not very good.
   B ~~The acting was terrible.~~
   C The story was too complicated.
   D It didn't make any sense.
   E ~~It was too long.~~

Option C mentions the 'story', but says it was too complicated, which does not match the text.

Option D is closest in meaning to the text — 'incomprehensible' means 'doesn't make any sense'.

3) <u>Double-check</u> you haven't <u>missed anything</u> else. The last line of the passage does suggest that the screenwriter was not very good (option A), but D is still the <u>best answer</u>.

Use Your Own Words *for Standard Answer Questions*

1) <u>Standard Answer comprehension questions</u> aren't <u>too different</u> from Multiple Choice questions.

2) You can find the answers in the <u>same way</u>, but instead of choosing a given answer, you need to put it into your <u>own words</u> and write in <u>full sentences</u>.

3) <u>Read</u> the <u>extract</u> on p.64, and then look at the question below.

 Q 2) Explain why the writer found the plot "incomprehensible" (line 2).

Method — Ask yourself questions as you're reading

1) First, work out <u>what information</u> the question is asking you for:

> Explain why the writer found the plot "incomprehensible" (line 2)?

This gives you a clue to where to start looking for the answer.

This tells you that you're looking for reasons why the writer didn't understand the story.

2) You should <u>start</u> by looking at the part of the text <u>mentioned</u> in the <u>question</u>:

> I have no idea what Captain Jutter had to do with anything, partly because I could not understand a word he said, but also because he disappeared halfway through the film, without any explanation.

This sentence comes straight after the writer mentions that the story was "incomprehensible".

Finding key words will help you work out what's important.

This sentence tells you that the writer <u>did not know why</u> Captain Jutter was in the film, because he <u>could not understand</u> what he said, and he <u>disappeared</u> halfway through.

3) After looking around line 2, you should then <u>check</u> the <u>key words</u> in the <u>rest of the text</u>:

> I don't think it was ever explained exactly why the pirates had to get back to Shadow Island...

The word 'explained' suggests that this sentence relates to the plot.

4) After you have <u>all the information</u>, you need to <u>rewrite</u> it in <u>full sentences</u>, in your <u>own words</u>:

> The plot was "incomprehensible" because the writer did not know why Captain Jutter was in the film, and found it impossible to understand him. The writer was also confused because Captain Jutter vanished in the middle of the film, and it was not explained why the pirates needed to go to Shadow Island.

Quoting from the question helps focus your answer.

Change the wording so you're not just copying the text.

5) Use the <u>number of marks</u> and <u>space available</u> for your answer as a guide for <u>how much</u> to write.

Tips and Tricks for Comprehension Questions

Try to answer every question. If you're not really sure what the answer is, make a sensible guess at it because you might still get it right. Don't spend too long on one question though — you need to use your time wisely.

Section Five — Comprehension

Comprehension Question Practice

Now that you know about answering comprehension questions, it's time for some practice.
There are some Multiple Choice and Standard Answer questions on the next page.

Q Read the passage and then answer the following questions.

1   *The small boys rushed in again. Closing, they saw, was their best chance, and Flashman*
     was wilder and more flurried than ever: he caught East by the throat, and tried to force him back
     on the iron-bound table. Tom grasped his waist, and remembering the old throw he
     had learned in the Vale from Harry Winburn, crooked his leg inside Flashman's, and threw

5   *his whole weight forward. The three tottered for a moment, and then over they went on to*
     the floor, Flashman striking his head against a form in the hall.
     The two youngsters sprang to their legs, but he lay there still. They began to be frightened.
     Tom stooped down, and then cried out, scared out of his wits, "He's bleeding awfully.
     Come here, East, Diggs — he's dying!"

10   *"Not he," said Diggs, getting leisurely off the table; "it's all sham; he's only afraid to fight it out."*
     East was as frightened as Tom. Diggs lifted Flashman's head, and he groaned.
     "What's the matter?" shouted Diggs.
     "My skull's fractured," sobbed Flashman.
     "Oh, let me run for the housekeeper!" cried Tom. "What shall we do?"

15   *"Fiddlesticks! It's nothing but the skin broken," said the relentless Diggs, feeling his head.*
     "Cold water and a bit of rag's all he'll want."
     "Let me go," said Flashman surlily, sitting up; "I don't want your help."
     "We're really very sorry —" began East.
     "Hang your sorrow!" answered Flashman, holding his handkerchief to the place;

20   *"you shall pay for this, I can tell you, both of you." And he walked out of the hall.*
     "He can't be very bad," said Tom with a deep sigh, much relieved to see his enemy march so well.
     "Not he," said Diggs; "and you'll see you won't be troubled with him any more.
     But, I say, your head's broken too; your collar is covered with blood."
     "Is it though?" said Tom, putting up his hand; "I didn't know it."

25   *"Well, mop it up, or you'll have your jacket spoilt. And you have got a nasty eye, Scud.*
     You'd better go and bathe it well in cold water."
     "Cheap enough too, if we've done with our old friend Flashey," said East, as they made off
     upstairs to bathe their wounds.
     They had done with Flashman in one sense, for he never laid finger on either of them again.

     From 'Tom Brown's Schooldays' by Thomas Hughes

Multiple Choice Practice

1) Which word best describes Flashman's mood at the start of the passage?

   A Panicked   **B** Tired   **C** Upset   **D** Frenzied   **E** Confused

2) According to the passage, which statement is true?

   A Diggs was involved in the fight.
   B Tom is the school bully.
   C Scud is the same person as East.
   D Harry is a good fighter.
   E Flashman fractures his skull.

3) Which word is closest in meaning to "relentless" (line 15)?

   A Vicious   **B** Persistent   **C** Boring   **D** Hardworking   **E** Stupid

4) Which word is closest in meaning to "surlily" (line 17)?

   A Dizzily   **B** Politely   **C** Violently   **D** Sadly   **E** Grumpily

5) What does Tom mean when he says, "He can't be very bad" (line 21)?

   A Flashman is not very popular.
   B Flashman is a nice person.
   C Flashman has only a minor injury.
   D Flashman is not very good at fighting.
   E Flashman is worried about getting into trouble.

6) Who is Tom's "enemy" (line 21)?

   A The housekeeper   **B** Diggs   **C** Harry Winburn   **D** Flashey   **E** Scud

Standard Answer Practice

1) Look again at lines 7-15. How does the writer show the anxiety of the characters?

2) Explain the meaning of the phrase "Cheap enough too" (line 27) as it is used in the text.

3) Whose side do you think the writer wants his readers to take? Explain your answer.

4) What kind of mood does the writer create in the last line of the passage?

How to Prepare for the Writing Test

Most people find creative writing tricky — follow the advice in this section and you'll be fine.

Work on your *Vocabulary* and *Writing Style*

Here are some ways you can <u>improve</u> your <u>writing style</u> before the test:

1) <u>Read</u> lots of books to develop your <u>vocab</u> and <u>writing style</u>.
   Read a <u>range</u> of things — <u>fiction</u>, <u>non-fiction</u> and <u>poetry</u>.

2) Write <u>vocabulary lists</u> of <u>tricky words</u> and their <u>meanings</u> — advanced vocabulary
   will help you to <u>impress</u> the examiners (as long as you use it <u>correctly</u>).

3) Make a list of <u>useful techniques</u> — e.g. <u>comparison</u> (see p.75) and <u>personification</u> (see p.49).
   Write down some <u>examples</u> of each to help you remember <u>how to use them</u>.

4) You could also jot down some <u>useful phrases</u> that you could use in almost any story. For example,
   <u>general descriptions</u> of <u>surroundings</u> — 'a quilted forest floor' or 'a picture of tranquillity'.

When you come across a word you don't know, look it up in a dictionary.

Prepare some *Ideas Before* the *Test*

1) Some <u>topics</u> come up often in the test. It will <u>save you time</u> if you've already thought about
   these — even if your question is different, you can <u>adapt</u> the stories you've <u>prepared</u>.

Prepare a basic *Structure* and *Plot* for these *Common Themes*

If you're asked to continue an extract from a story, make sure that you copy the style of the text as closely as you can.

Achieving or doing something exciting	Having an adventure
Being in the city or the countryside	Holidays
What you want to be when you grow up	Being lost, scared or alone

Think of *Characters* and *Settings* to include in your *Writing*

1) Here are some ideas for <u>characters</u> you could use in lots of <u>different stories</u>:

| A kind old lady | A strict teacher | A sporty teenager | A brave child |

2) Have a think about <u>different settings</u> too — your story could take place in:

| A haunted house | A busy city | A desert island | An empty school |

3) <u>Picture</u> the character or place in your mind — think about what you can <u>see</u> and how you'd
   <u>describe</u> it. Think of some <u>comparisons</u> to make your descriptions <u>interesting</u> (see p.75),
   e.g. 'her fingers were like gnarled twigs' or 'The island was an emerald in a sapphire sea.'

2) Think of some ways to <u>start</u> and <u>end</u> a story too — you could <u>start</u> in the middle of the <u>action</u> to
   grab your reader's attention, and you could <u>end</u> with something <u>unexpected</u> (see p.70).

Read plenty of Non-fiction Texts

1) You might have to write a <u>non-fiction</u> text in the test — for example, a <u>letter</u> or <u>newspaper article</u>.

2) To help you prepare, <u>read</u> lots of non-fiction texts, for example <u>adverts</u>, <u>articles</u> in newspapers and magazines, and <u>books</u> about <u>history</u> or <u>science</u>.

Think about whether the Writer is trying to:

1) <u>Persuade</u> you to do something (e.g. <u>donate</u> money, <u>buy</u> a product).

> It is vital that these cats find a loving home. Haven't they suffered enough?

Persuasive writing contains arguments. It might try to appeal to the reader's emotions.

2) <u>Inform</u> you about a subject (e.g. a natural history book might tell you about dinosaurs).

> Dinosaurs died out 65 million years ago, so scientists use fossils to learn about them.

Informative writing contains facts. It might give numbers or statistics.

3) <u>Describe</u> something (e.g. a travel journal might describe a foreign country).

> The soft lights of Copenhagen glittered like jewels across the darkening sea as our ship neared shore.

Descriptive writing is full of adjectives. It often goes into a lot of detail.

3) Use what you've read to <u>help</u> you with your <u>own non-fiction writing</u>. Think about what you're asked to write and whether you should <u>persuade</u>, <u>inform</u> or <u>describe</u> something to your reader.

Practise writing Letters

You might well be asked to write a <u>letter</u> in the test. Letters are just like <u>any other</u> type of writing, but you have to use the <u>right style</u>, and know how to <u>start</u> and <u>end</u> them properly.

Letters can be Formal or Informal

1) Letters to people you <u>don't know well</u>, or somebody <u>in charge</u>, should use a <u>formal style</u>.

These are both formal introductions.

| Dear Sir/Madam | ⟹ | Yours faithfully |
| Dear Mrs Jones | ⟹ | Yours sincerely |

These are both formal endings.

Use 'Yours sincerely' if you use their name, 'Yours faithfully' if you don't.

2) Letters to a <u>friend</u> or <u>relative</u> should use an <u>informal style</u>.

This is an informal introduction.

| Dear Tony | ⟹ | Best wishes | or | See you soon |

These are both informal endings.

Get some practice at writing <u>informal</u> letters — you could write to <u>relatives</u> or to a <u>penpal</u> in another country, and <u>formal</u> letters — for example to your <u>local council</u> to give your <u>views</u> on an <u>issue</u> such as the closure of a youth club or library.

Formal writing isn't too chatty and uses standard English. Informal writing is more chatty — as though you're talking to your reader.

Make a Plan

Like anything in life, it's important to have a good plan. 11+ English is no different...

Stories should have a Beginning, Middle and End

If you're writing a <u>story</u>, make sure you <u>structure</u> it clearly:

> *Writing a plan (see p.71) will help you work out the best structure for your story or essay.*

1) <u>Beginning</u> — your first paragraph has to <u>grab</u> the reader's <u>attention</u>.

You could start by <u>setting</u> the <u>scene</u>... → It was a cold, dark November evening.

... or you could jump straight into the <u>action</u>. → The beast attacked again that night, leaving chaos in its wake.

2) <u>Middle</u> — build up your <u>action</u>. Make sure you've got at least <u>one key event</u> in your <u>plan</u> that you can <u>describe</u> in detail. Don't forget to write in <u>paragraphs</u> (see p.72).

Suddenly I heard a pattering behind me. I spun around, and found myself looking into the glinting, red eyes of the beast. ← Make sure enough <u>happens</u> to keep your reader hooked, but don't forget to make your descriptions <u>interesting</u>.

3) <u>End</u> — make sure your story <u>finishes</u> with a paragraph that <u>wraps up</u> your plot.

You could end with a <u>twist</u> to surprise your reader... → "There you are, Snowy," I said, scooping up my pet rabbit.

... or you could <u>reflect</u> on what your character has <u>learnt</u>. → From that day, Kieran was a changed boy. He became kind and thoughtful, and he never bullied anyone again.

Essays should have an Introduction, Argument and Conclusion

<u>Structure</u> is just as important if you're writing a <u>non-fiction</u> text, like an <u>essay</u>, <u>letter</u> or <u>article</u>:

1) <u>Introduction</u> — your first paragraph should <u>explain</u> what you're going to write about.

Put forward your <u>main argument</u>... → Unhealthy food should not be sold in schools because it causes obesity.

... or if you're writing to <u>inform</u>, <u>introduce</u> your topic. → Durham is an ancient city in north-east England.

2) <u>Argument</u> — use the middle of the essay to <u>back up</u> your points and give <u>detail</u>.

More than 25% of children in the UK are overweight, and 6% say that they are bullied because of their weight. ← If you're writing to <u>persuade</u>, use <u>statistics</u> to make your argument <u>convincing</u>.

3) <u>Conclusion</u> — use your last paragraph to <u>summarise</u> your points.

Writing 'In conclusion' or 'In summary' makes it clear that this is the <u>end</u> of your essay. → In conclusion, if schools stopped selling unhealthy food then children would be healthier and happier, and would grow into healthy adults.

Write a **Plan** to **Structure** your **Answer**

Planning your essay will help you to structure your writing and write a better answer. The amount of time you spend planning will depend on the overall time limit for the writing task.

Q Write a story about an unusual event.

Read the question carefully — pick out what type of writing it's asking for, and what the topic is.

Method — Write a brief plan using bullet points

1) If you're short of time in the test, your plan should be very short.

2) Look at the question and spend a couple of minutes working out what you want to write about.

3) Write your plan in note form — jot down a point for your beginning, a few points for the middle and a point for the end.

> • <u>Beginning</u> — Quiet evening, baby-sitting sister
> • <u>Middle</u> — Roof collapsed — noise, dust, scary
>   House dangerous — went to neighbours
>   Investigation — roof hit by satellite
> • <u>End</u> — Government paid, house nicer now!

Write in note form to save time.

Q Write a story (real or made up) with the title 'Lost and Alone'.

Method — Use a spider diagram to plan your answer

1) If you've got more time, your essay will be longer, so your plan needs to be more detailed.

2) Decide what you're going to write about, then jot down your ideas as notes or a spider diagram.

3) Spider diagrams are a good way to see how different ideas are connected.

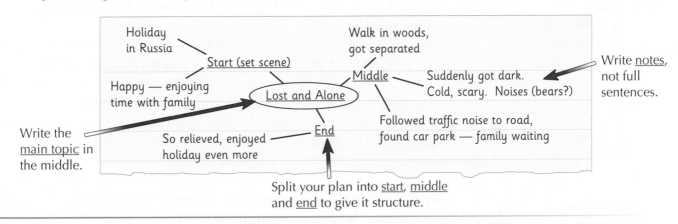

Write <u>notes</u>, not full sentences.

Write the <u>main topic</u> in the middle.

Split your plan into <u>start</u>, <u>middle</u> and <u>end</u> to give it structure.

Practice Questions

1) Write down a plan of five bullet points for each of the questions below.

   a) *Write an article arguing that driving lessons should be given at secondary school.*

   b) *Write a story with 'A Surprise Party' as the title.*

Section Six — Writing

Write in Paragraphs

Make sure you know how to use paragraphs correctly — just follow these simple rules.

Warm-Up Activity

1) Get your favourite fiction book and open it up at the beginning of the story.
2) Count how many paragraphs there are on the first two pages.
3) Write down why you think each new paragraph is started.
   For example, 'a new character is introduced'.

Use **Paragraphs** to **Introduce Something New**

1) A paragraph is a group of sentences that talk about the same thing, or follow on from each other.
2) All of the sentences in a paragraph should be related to each other.
3) Start a new paragraph every time something changes.

When something new happens, you start a new paragraph.

...in the light of the full moon.
      The whole camp was quiet as Brutus sat alone in his tent. He couldn't sleep, nor could he stop thinking about Portia. Why did she have to die?
      Then he heard something — something strange, like a distant whispering sound...

The ideas in this paragraph are related. This paragraph is about Brutus sitting in his tent.

Learn When to Use a New Paragraph

Start a New Paragraph When...

A different person is speaking.

"I'll find him," muttered Donald. "He won't get away this time, wherever he hides."
      Mickey raised his eyebrows. "What makes you so sure?" he asked.
"What's going on here?" demanded a voice from the darkness.

The story changes to a different place.

The playing fields were peaceful and there was no one around except Pete. He listened to the birds singing and sighed happily.
      Back in the classroom, Mr Jackson was staring at Pete's empty chair and wondering why he was late for French.

The story changes to a different time.

By five o'clock, Edwin was angry. Shirley was late again, and the flower he'd bought was starting to droop.
      Six o'clock came, and she still hadn't appeared. Enough was enough. Stuffing his flower into a bin, Edwin went home.

The action of the story changes

Lauren kicked her feet through the dead leaves and reached down to pick up a stick to throw for Barney. It was then that she heard it.
      The growl of a motorbike engine could clearly be heard approaching along the path through the woods.

Section Six — Writing

Make sure that you **Show New Paragraphs Clearly**

Q Rewrite the text below, putting in new paragraphs where they belong.

Emily stood at the side of the court, watching her team slump to another defeat. As soon as the half-time buzzer went, she stormed into the dressing room. The players watched her leave. "She doesn't look too happy," commented Harriet, the team's top scorer. As the team entered the dressing room, Emily was pacing up and down, muttering to herself. "Pathetic. Pathetic!" she shouted at the team as they sat down. Fifteen minutes later, the team came back on the court. Perhaps this time Emily's half-time talk would make a difference.

Method — Look for things that change

1) Read through the passage <u>one sentence</u> at a time, working out where new paragraphs belong.

The first sentence should begin a paragraph.

Harriet is a new speaker.

// Emily stood at the side of the court, watching her team slump to another defeat. As soon as the half-time buzzer went, she stormed into the dressing room. The players watched her leave.// "She doesn't look too happy," commented Harriet, the team's top scorer.//As the team entered the dressing room, Emily was pacing up and down, muttering to herself. "Pathetic. Pathetic!" she shouted at the team as they sat down.//Fifteen minutes later, the team came back on the court. Perhaps this time Emily's half-time talk would make a difference.

The dressing room is a new place.

This is a new time.

2) Once you work out where the <u>new paragraphs should start</u>, you can <u>rewrite</u> the passage. Show new paragraphs by <u>starting</u> a <u>new line</u> and <u>leaving a small gap before</u> the <u>first sentence</u>.

Add a space at the beginning of the paragraph.

...watched her leave.
    "She doesn't look too happy," commented Harriet, the team's top scorer.

Start a new line.

Practice Questions

1) Divide this text into paragraphs. Write // where a new paragraph should start.

Following another run-in with Mr Ulrichson, Gary had awaited his verdict nervously. "Gary, this is the third time you've been brought to my office for being late. I would have thought a 17 year old like you would know better," the headmaster said, "but I think I know the perfect punishment — Mr Levis needs some help with the junior hockey team and I remember you used to be very good at hockey, you might even enjoy it." That was three weeks ago, and since then Gary had been coming to the threadbare pitch every week to help with the coaching. This was a task he didn't enjoy — he disliked the children and he despised standing in the cold watching them play hockey. There was one child he truly hated: Wesley Fenton. Wesley had been a nuisance right from the start. He enjoyed tying Gary's shoelaces together when he wasn't looking and took every opportunity to hit the ball as hard as he could at Gary. "Stupid kids!" thought Gary, as it started to rain again. "Stupid, rotten, silly kids!"

Make It Interesting

Your reader likes an interesting story as much as the next person — so make it interesting.

Don't Use the Same Words over and over again

Use different words with similar meanings to make your writing interesting (see p.56-57).

Different Adjectives

See p.12 for more on adjectives.

1) Adjectives are a good way to make your writing interesting, but using the same adjectives, like 'weird' or 'nice', gets repetitive:

> I went to a nice Indian restaurant last night. I had an onion bhaji to start with and it was really nice. Then I had a nice curry.

This is written correctly, but repeating the word 'nice' makes it boring.

2) Using different adjectives makes all the difference:

> I went to a great Indian restaurant last night. I had an onion bhaji to start with and it was really tasty. Then I had a delicious curry.

This is the same piece of writing, but it's much more interesting.

Different Verbs

See p.10 for more on verbs.

Using different verbs that mean similar things will make your writing more interesting than if you use the same ones over and over again.

> I ran to the postbox with a letter, then I ran home so I wasn't late for tea.

> I hurried to the postbox with a letter, then I raced home so I wasn't late for tea.

These sentences are better because the verbs are more interesting. The verbs have slightly different meanings, but the stories stay the same.

> He jumped through the open window, and then jumped over the sleeping dog.

> He leaped through the open window, and then bounded over the sleeping dog.

Different Connectives

See p.14 for more on connectives.

1) Don't use the same connectives all the time. You can avoid using 'and' or 'then' by using different punctuation, such as commas and full stops:

> I went to the beach and I put on my trunks and I walked to the sea and the water was warm and I swam for an hour.

> I went to the beach, put on my trunks and walked to the sea. The water was warm and I swam for an hour.

2) You could also use different connectives or change the order of the words:

> We went to the bank then we had a coffee, then we went back to the car. Then we drove to the supermarket to do some shopping.

> After going to the bank, we had a coffee. Then we went back to the car and drove to the supermarket to do some shopping.

Comparisons *can create* Clear Imagery

1) <u>Comparisons</u> help the reader to <u>picture</u> something more <u>clearly</u>.

| It was very cold. | ⟹ | It was colder than an Arctic winter. | ⟸ This helps you imagine how cold it was. |

2) You can <u>exaggerate</u> (make something out to be <u>more</u> than it <u>really is</u>) to <u>stress</u> a <u>point</u>:

Jack is as tall as a tree. ⟸ Jack isn't really as tall as most trees, but your reader will understand, as long as your comparisons don't go over the top.

There are Two Main Ways *of* Comparing

Don't use 'more' and '-er' or 'most' and '-est' together, e.g. 'most tallest' — stick to one or the other.

Less Than, More Than

You can make a comparison by saying '<u>more ... than</u>', '<u>less ... than</u>', '<u>most</u>' or '<u>least</u>', or you can use the <u>form</u> of the <u>word</u> that ends in '<u>-er</u>' or '<u>-est</u>'.

| Ted is more sporty than Helen. | ⟹ | Ted is sport<u>ier</u> than Helen. |
| He is the most sporty person I know. | ⟹ | He is the sport<u>iest</u> person I know. |

Say that One Thing is Like Another

These are similes (see p.48) — using them will make your writing more interesting.

Another way of comparing is to say <u>one thing</u> is <u>like another</u>.

1) You can do this by using the word '<u>like</u>'.

| Her eyes lit up like the sky on bonfire night. | | Soon my fingers were like blocks of ice. |

2) You can also use '<u>as ... as</u>':

| He was as happy as a lark. | | The idea was as useless as a chocolate teapot. |

Learn *these* Useful Comparative Words

Words like 'best', 'worst' and 'most' are called superlatives.

Use these words to show how things are <u>related</u> to one another:

good		better		best	Balal is good at writing stories, but Sam is better.
bad		worse		worst	
much/many	⟹	more	⟹	most	Kell knows more card games than me, but Ali knows the most.
little		less		least	
few		fewer		fewest	Maria made few mistakes in the test, Leah made fewer than Maria, and I made the fewest.

Use **Different Types** of **Sentences**

1) Starting every sentence the <u>same way</u> can sound dull.
Begin each sentence in a <u>different way</u>:

This is much better.

| There was nobody around as Jo knocked on the door. There was a scream from inside. | ⇨ | Nobody was around as Jo knocked on the door. A scream came from inside. |

2) Use a variety of <u>long</u> and <u>short sentences</u>. <u>Short sentences</u> make descriptions sound <u>fast</u> and <u>exciting</u> whereas <u>long sentences</u> make descriptions sound <u>thoughtful</u> and <u>clever</u>:

| I was walking to the station. I needed to catch a train. It left at one. I was late. I decided to run. | These are too short. | I was walking to the station because I needed to catch a train which left at one, and I was late so I decided to run. | This is too long. |

| I was walking to the station because I needed to catch a train which left at one. I was late so I decided to run. | This is a good mix of long and short. |

Add or **Replace Words** to make your **Sentences Better**

> **Q** Without changing the meaning of each sentence, add or replace at least two words to make the sentences more interesting.
>
> a) *We stayed inside because of the weather.*
> b) *"That sounds like a deal!" said Mr Tibbs.*

Method — Think of synonyms or adjectives

a) We stayed inside because of the terrible icy weather. ⇐ You could add some adjectives to this sentence.

b) "That sounds like a great deal!" exclaimed old Mr Tibbs. ⇐ You could replace the verb 'said' and add some adjectives to make this more interesting.

Practice Questions

1) Rewrite these sentences, adding at least two adjectives to make them more interesting.

   a) *They went out to the park and played on the swings, the slide and the roundabout.*
   b) *Mr Brown told his cats to stay inside, but they never listened to him.*
   c) *Johan said there was too much violence, aggression and shouting in the film.*

2) Replace the underlined words in these sentences to make them more interesting.

   a) *We <u>ate</u> all the sausages because we were <u>hungry</u>, but they tasted <u>bad</u>.*
   b) *I <u>ran</u> to the cinema, but it was so <u>dark</u> that I <u>fell</u> and <u>hurt</u> my knee.*
   c) *It was a <u>nice</u> evening, but even though they <u>liked</u> the play, they <u>disliked</u> the songs.*

Writing Practice

The best way to brush up on your writing skills is to practise — here are some questions to start you off.

Practice Questions — Writing Techniques

1) Rewrite these extracts to make them more interesting. Add or replace words, join together sentences that are too short and break up sentences that are too long.

   a) *It was a nice day. I walked to the beach. I made a sandcastle. I ate an ice cream.*

   b) *The ogre was ugly and I felt scared and so I hid behind a rock until he left.*

   c) *"Quick, give me the fishing rod!" I said. I had seen a movement under the water. "Here you go," said Timmy, throwing me the rod. "It might not be strong enough. The Loch Ness monster is big. Here, take the net as well."*

2) Write a comparison to say that each of these things is like something else.

   a) *The sky was like...*   b) *The meal was as hot as...*   c) *His hair was like...*

Practice Questions — Writing Fiction

1) Write five words to describe each of these characters:

   a) *an evil wizard.*   b) *a helpful lollipop man.*   c) *a talking bear.*

2) Now write a description of the place where each character in question (1) lives.

3) Write a plan for each of the following questions:

   a) *Write a short story with 'Extreme Weather' as the title.*

   b) *Read the extract on p.73 about Emily's half-time team talk. Continue the story from the end of the passage, explaining what happened next.*

4) Choose one of the questions from (3). Use your plan to help you write the full story.

Practice Questions — Writing Non-fiction

1) Write a plan for each of the following questions:

   a) *Write a letter to a friend informing them about the pros and cons of owning a pet.*

   b) *Write a letter to your headteacher arguing against pupils having to wear uniforms.*

   c) *Write a journal entry describing what you did on your holidays.*

2) Choose one of the questions from (1). Use your plan to help you write the full essay.

Tips and Tricks for the Writing Test

If you have time at the end, read through what you've written and correct any mistakes.

Glossary

abbreviation	A <u>shortened version</u> of a word, e.g. "<u>bike</u>" instead of "bicycle".
acronym	A word formed from the <u>initial letters</u> of a name or by combining initial letters of a series of words, e.g. "<u>NATO</u>" (North Atlantic Treaty Organisation).
adjective	A word that <u>describes</u> a <u>noun</u>, e.g. "<u>beautiful</u> morning", "<u>frosty</u> lawn".
adverb	A word that <u>describes</u> a <u>verb</u> or an <u>adjective</u>, e.g. "she spoke <u>loudly</u>", "he ran <u>quickly</u>".
alliteration	The <u>repetition</u> of a <u>sound</u> at the beginning of words within a phrase, e.g. "<u>L</u>oopy <u>L</u>ois <u>l</u>ikes <u>l</u>ipstick."
antonym	A word that has the <u>opposite meaning</u> to another, e.g. "good" and "bad".
comparative	A word that <u>compares</u> one thing with another, e.g. "<u>shorter</u>", "<u>worse</u>".
connective	A word that <u>joins</u> two clauses or sentences, e.g. "<u>and</u>", "<u>but</u>", "<u>therefore</u>".
fiction	Text that has been <u>made up</u> by the author, about <u>imaginary people</u> and <u>events</u>.
homographs	Words that are <u>spelt the same</u>, but have <u>different meanings</u>, e.g. <u>row</u> (argue/paddle).
homophones	Words that <u>sound the same</u>, but mean different things, e.g. "<u>hair</u>" and "<u>hare</u>".
idiom	A phrase which <u>doesn't literally mean</u> what it <u>says</u>, e.g. "raining cats and dogs".
imagery	Language that creates a <u>vivid picture</u> in the reader's mind.
irony	When a writer says the <u>opposite</u> of what they <u>mean</u>, or when the <u>opposite happens</u> to what the reader <u>expects</u>.
metaphor	A way of <u>describing</u> something by saying that it <u>is</u> something else, e.g. "John's legs were lead weights."
non-fiction	Text that is about <u>facts</u> and <u>real people</u> and <u>events</u>.
noun	A word that <u>names</u> something, e.g. "<u>Paul</u>", "<u>scissors</u>", "<u>flock</u>", "<u>loyalty</u>".
onomatopoeia	When words <u>sound</u> like the <u>noise</u> they describe, e.g. "<u>pop</u>", "<u>bang</u>", "<u>squelch</u>".
personification	A way of describing something by giving it <u>human feelings</u> and <u>characteristics</u>, e.g. "The cruel wind plucked remorselessly at my threadbare clothes."
prefix	Letters that can be put <u>in front</u> of a word to <u>change its meaning</u>, e.g. "<u>un</u>lock".
preposition	A word that tells you how things are <u>related</u>, e.g. "<u>in</u>", "<u>above</u>", "<u>before</u>", "<u>of</u>".
pronoun	Words that can be used <u>instead</u> of <u>nouns</u>, e.g. "<u>I</u>", "<u>you</u>", "<u>he</u>", "<u>it</u>".
rhetorical question	A question that <u>doesn't</u> need an <u>answer</u>, e.g. "When will they learn?"
simile	A way of describing something by <u>comparing</u> it to something else, e.g. "The stars were <u>like</u> a thousand diamonds, glittering in the sky."
subject	The <u>person</u> or <u>thing doing</u> the action of a verb, e.g. "<u>Jo</u> laughed", "<u>the bird</u> flew".
suffix	Letters that can be put <u>after</u> a word to <u>change its meaning</u>, e.g. "play<u>ful</u>" .
superlative	A word that refers to the <u>most</u> or <u>least</u> of a group of things, e.g. "the <u>best</u> team".
synonym	A word with a <u>similar meaning</u> to another word, e.g. "<u>big</u>" and "<u>huge</u>".
verb	An <u>action</u> or <u>being</u> word, e.g. "I <u>run</u>", "he <u>went</u>", "you <u>are</u>", "we <u>think</u>".

Answers

PAGES 4-6 — SENTENCES AND CLAUSES

Warm-Up Activity

Some examples are:

You have to be up early tomorrow to play your violin.

Let's go birdwatching and eat frogs' legs.

Practice Questions

1) a) Before I go to bed, <u>I always brush my teeth</u>.
   b) In three months' time, <u>the gardener is retiring</u>.
   c) <u>Bruce can't go swimming</u> because he's got an upset stomach.
   d) <u>We'll eat now</u>, and then go for a run.

The words that are underlined make up the main clause.

2) a) Complex sentence.
   b) Compound sentence.
   c) Complex sentence.
   d) Compound sentence.

Compound sentences contain clauses that each make sense on their own. Complex sentences contain clauses that don't make sense on their own.

PAGES 7-9 — NOUNS AND PRONOUNS

Warm-Up Activity

'bunch' = 'grapes'   'litter' = 'kittens'   'caravan' = 'camels'
'shoal' = 'fish'   'flock' = 'sheep'

Practice Questions

1) a) 'swarm' is a collective noun.
   b) 'December' is a proper noun.
   c) 'Scotland' is a proper noun.
   d) 'cauliflower' is a common noun.
   e) 'lady' is a common noun.
   f) 'ostrich' is a common noun.
   g) 'class' is a collective noun.
   h) 'hockey' is a common noun.
   i) 'Sue' and 'Shaw' are both proper nouns.

Proper nouns are names; collective nouns are words for groups of things; common nouns are words for types of things.

2) Helen and Yasmin swam desperately towards the island in the distance, although **it** wasn't getting any closer. After a while, **they** felt their feet touch the sandy shore and **they** knew that they had made it. Helen looked around and **she** saw a completely deserted paradise which had never been visited by humans before. Yasmin saw a tree heavily laden with fruit a short distance away. "Come on Helen," **she** said. "Let's get something to eat."

The words in bold show where pronouns have replaced nouns.

PAGES 10-11 — VERBS

1) a) The concert **starts** in ten minutes' time.
   b) We **finished** our fun run in record time, despite the bird costumes.
   c) John **perfected** the decorations on the birthday cake.
   d) I **love** rock-climbing in the Lake District during the summer.

e) Christmas **brings** increased business to many toy shops.
f) The steam train **rushes** past on its way to the coast.

The words in bold are the verbs — remember the verbs are action words or being words.

2) a) Barney has **eaten** all of my popcorn.
   b) I have **been** to South Africa on holiday.
   c) Barry's knee is **hurting** after he fell over.
   d) You should **go** home or you'll be late.
   e) What time do you think you will **arrive**?
   f) The dolphin is about to **leap** out of the water.

Read the sentence out loud to help you find the right answer.

PAGES 12-13 — ADJECTIVES, ADVERBS AND PREPOSITIONS

1) a) 'funnier' is a comparative.
   b) 'strangest' is a superlative.
   c) 'most graceful' is a superlative.
   d) 'bizarre' is an adjective.
   e) 'joyful' is an adjective.
   f) 'less fascinating' is a comparative.

Comparatives often end in 'er' and superlatives often end in 'st'.

2) a) Chris closed his eyes **nervously** as the shuttle started to move. (adverb)
   b) Joyce leant over to tell Anupreet to try the **crispy** potato skins. (adjective)
   c) Molly looked **around** the side of the lorry to check for traffic. (preposition)
   d) I was the **only** child waiting to be collected after school. (adjective)
   e) Carrie **gladly** accepted the offer of a place to stay. (adverb)
   f) When Mum shouted at Terry, he crawled **under** the table to sulk. (preposition)

The words in bold are the part of speech you need to identify.

PAGES 14-15 — CONNECTIVES

1) The Amazon Rainforest covers 40% of South America, <u>although</u> it has decreased in size. Humans have cut down the trees <u>because</u> they need wood for construction <u>and</u> space for farms <u>and</u> roads. <u>However</u>, conservation efforts are under way to protect the rainforest <u>and</u> stop people from illegally cutting down the trees.

The words that are underlined are the connectives.

2) a) I really like to eat cereal for breakfast. **However**, I sometimes eat a slice of toast.
   b) I'd like to go out to the Italian restaurant tonight, **although** Chinese is my favourite.
   c) We went to play hockey, **despite** the rain.

Look at the context to find the correct connective.

PAGES 16-19 — ANSWERING GRAMMAR QUESTIONS

1) a) The connectives are 'and' and 'However'.
   b) 'desperate' is an adjective because it describes Harriet.
   c) 'angrily' is an adverb.

You'll need to think about the different parts of speech to identify the correct answer.

PAGES 20-22 — STARTING AND ENDING SENTENCES

1) **a)** Look out — it's the mutant cheesecake!
   b) Does this hat make my ears look funny?

You always begin a sentence with a capital letter, but you need to read the whole sentence before you know what to add to the end.

2) **a) - d)** Various answers possible.

Make sure you've used all the types of punctuation correctly.

3) **1** Peter Handy was a fisherman. Every day he went out on his boat in the bay to
   2 catch fish. One day he went down to the dock as usual to find his boat missing**.**
   3 "Oh dear!" cried Peter. "What am I going to do now**?**"
   4 He sat down on the dock and put his head in his hands. But just then**...**

Line 1 contains no errors. Line 2 needs a full stop at the end of the line after the word 'missing', whilst line 3 needs a question mark before the second set of speech marks close. Line 4 ends on a cliffhanger, so an ellipsis should be used at the end of the line.

PAGES 23-25 — COMMAS, DASHES AND BRACKETS

1) **a)** Subia didn't want to go fishing with her dad**,** but he'd brought the equipment.
   b) Ravens**,** pigeons and seagulls were Nicci's least favourite types of bird.
   c) Albert ran for his train**,** but he was already four minutes late.
   d) Although they couldn't hear**,** George shouted angrily at the boys as they ran away.

It can be difficult to add commas that separate different clauses — look out for connectives, and for where you need to pause so that the sentence makes sense.

2) **Gareth and Lucy** were sick of their P.E. teacher**,** Mr Oden. Every day he made them do high jump, shot-put, **rugby and football**. One day they came up with a cunning plan **(along with the other children)** to get revenge on Mr Oden. They took all of the studs **out of** his football boots **(they stole them from under his desk)** so that when he put them on and started running**,** he fell head first into the mud.

There are 10 missing pieces of punctuation — make sure you've spotted them all and they're all in the right place.

PAGES 26-27 — APOSTROPHES

Warm-Up Activity

Some examples are:

Julia's kitten wouldn't walk down the stairs.

You're behaving as if it's my fault.

Practice Questions

1) **a)** Megan's goalkeeper jersey **wasn't** going to dry in time for her match.
   b) "There's no way that you're going out when **it's** this cold," shouted Zac's mum.
   c) **Marco's** new computer game was taking its time to arrive.
   d) Beatrice suddenly realised that she'd left her homework at her **dad's** house.
   e) The **policemen's** boots were covered in mud from the garden.

Look out for clues in the sentence, like words ending in 's' that might show possession.

2) **Fred's** room was definitely haunted. Every night he could hear a ghostly whistling coming from inside his wardrobe. One night, the wardrobe door started to rock noisily on **its** base. Fred leapt out of bed and called for **his** mum to come and investigate the wardrobe. She slowly opened the door to reveal Fred's sister hiding inside. "That **wasn't** funny," yelled Fred, as his sister rolled around laughing on the floor.

Use apostrophes to show where words have been shortened, e.g. 'wasn't', or to show possession, e.g. 'Fred's'. 'Its' only has an apostrophe when it means 'it is' or 'it has' before a verb.

PAGES 28-29 — SPEECH

1) **a)** "Listen carefully," said Matt, as he told them about the wizard's warning.
   b) Alex screamed into the night air, "Why can't I find the way?"
   c) "I need three starters, two desserts and one drink," shouted the waiter.

Speech marks should only contain the words that are spoken.

2) **a)** "How many people are coming?" asked Giles.
   b) Helen asked, "Will you have time to visit Maggie, George? I'm too busy."
   c) "Take some sun cream!" shouted Heidi. "It's sweltering out there."

Whenever you add speech marks to a sentence, think about where they should go in relation to the other punctuation.

PAGES 30-31 — COLONS AND SEMICOLONS

1) Pierre was very excited: it was the end of term. He was going to Greece on holiday the very next day. Pierre was looking forward to swimming in the bright blue **sea; browsing** the local Greek markets, looking for souvenirs; playing tennis at the **hotel; and** paying a visit to Athens. He didn't want to go to any **museums; his** mum would probably make him go anyway.

The first error is in the third sentence — a semicolon should be used instead of a colon to separate items in a list. The second error is at the end of the third sentence — there should be a semicolon before 'and'. The third error is in the final sentence — a semicolon should be used instead of a colon after 'museums' because the second clause does not explain what comes before it.

2) **a)** I've worked really hard; I expect to pass my exams.
   b) I never miss a football match; I'm the top scorer in the team.
   c) I went to the market for a new hat, but they didn't have any; I'll be back on Monday.
   d) I would like to thank my mum, who inspired me to sing; my teacher, who taught me how to hit the high notes; and my partner, who wrote me some great songs.

Two semicolons should be added to the final sentence to separate the items in the list.

PAGES 34-35 — PLURALS

1) **a)** The plural of 'branch' is 'branches'.
   b) The plural of 'tooth' is 'teeth'.
   c) The plural of 'Grady' is 'Gradys'.
   d) The plural of 'daisy' is 'daisies'.
   e) The plural of 'dress' is 'dresses'.

Words ending with 'ch' or 's' usually take an 'es' plural, and words ending with 'y' usually take an 'ies' plural unless it is a proper noun.

PAGES 36-37 — HOMOPHONES AND HOMOGRAPHS

Warm-Up Activity

'piece' sounds like 'peace'.
'waist' sounds like 'waste'.
'or' sounds like 'oar' and 'ore'.
'sale' sounds like 'sail'.
'sight' sounds like 'site' and 'cite'.
'male' sounds like 'mail'.

Practice Questions

1) I'm supposed to go to drama group every Monday **night**, but this **week** I'm too tired. I've had a very busy day at school and I'm not feeling **great**. Instead, I think I'm going to stay **here** and watch a film that I haven't **seen** before.

The words in bold are the correct homophones.

2) a) Make sure that you know **where** you are going.
    b) Watch out for the crab — it has very sharp **claws**.
    c) At the theme park, we **rode** on four different roller coasters.
    d) The jockey pulled on the **reins** to get the horse to stop.

The correct answer should have a meaning which fits the context.

PAGES 38-39 — PREFIXES AND SUFFIXES

Warm-Up Activity

'un' and 'available' make 'unavailable'.
'thought' and 'ful' make 'thoughtful'.
'formal' and 'ly' make 'formally'.
'work' and 'er' make 'worker'.

Practice Questions

1) a) The baby polar bear is so **adorable**.
    b) I was trying to be **helpful** when I washed the dishes.
    c) The ball hit Kayley and knocked her **unconscious**.
    d) Lyla's feeling of **happiness** increased when she found her shoes.
    e) The apple was covered in mould and the flesh was **rotten**.

The prefix and suffixes which have been added all fit the context of the sentences.

PAGES 40-41 — SILENT LETTERS AND DOUBLE LETTERS

Warm-Up Activity

In 'knife' the silent consonant is 'k'.
In 'scene' the silent consonant is 'c'.
In 'gnome' the silent consonant is 'g'.
In 'island' the silent consonant is 's'.
In 'while' the silent consonant is 'h'.
In 'lamb' the silent consonant is 'b'.
In 'rhyme' the silent consonant is 'h'.

Practice Questions

1) a) I **maintained** a comfortable position for the whole journey.
    b) You need to wear more **clothes** in winter to keep warm.
    c) My **interesting** entry will win the competition tomorrow.

Make sure that double letters have been used correctly.

2) a) Everyone agreed that the charity event had been **successful**.
    b) While we're in London, we want to visit Nelson's **Column**.
    c) Sasha is the most **intelligent** girl in the class.
    d) I arrived just as the show was **beginning**.

These are the correct spellings of each word.

PAGES 42-43 — OTHER AWKWARD SPELLINGS

1) a) My car is running out of **diesel**.
    b) Don't forget to paint the **ceiling**.
    c) Penny's **height** has increased by 9 cm this year.
    d) Mr Harris went to the museum to see the **ancient** remains.

Use the rule "'i' before 'e' except after 'c', but only when it rhymes with bee" to help you to work out the correct spellings.

2) a) The missing letter is 'e' in 'desp**e**rate'.
    b) The missing letter is 'o' in 'fact**o**ry'.
    c) The missing letter is 'i' in 'respons**i**ble'.
    d) The missing letter is 'o' in 'harm**o**ny'.
    e) The missing letters are 'e' and 'a' in 'lit**e**r**a**ture'.
    f) The missing letter is 'a' in 'pass**a**ge'.

These are the vowels needed to correctly spell each word.

PAGES 46-47 — ALLITERATION AND ONOMATOPOEIA

1) a) neither
    b) onomatopoeia — the word 'banged' is onomatopoeic.
    c) alliteration — the 's' sound is repeated.
    d) neither
    e) neither
    f) onomatopoeia — the word 'clucked' is onomatopoeic.

Think about the sounds used at the start of each word rather than the letters — if the same sound repeats, it's alliteration. If there's a word which sounds like the noise it's describing, it's onomatopoeia.

PAGES 48-50 — IMAGERY

1) a) personification — 'luck' is personified.
    b) simile — the phrase 'as ... as' shows that Fatima's clothes were like something else.
    c) personification — 'fear' is personified.
    d) simile — the phrase 'as ... as' shows that the packed classroom was like something else.
    e) metaphor — the sentence says that Gary's fingers 'were' something else.

If the sentence gives human qualities to anything other than a person, it's personification. If the sentence compares something to something else, it's an example of a simile. If the sentence says that something is something else then it's a metaphor.

PAGE 51 — ABBREVIATIONS

Warm-Up Activity

'Dr' is the abbreviation for 'Doctor'.
'sci-fi' is the abbreviation for 'science fiction'.
'FC' is the abbreviation for 'Football Club'.
'ttyl' is the abbreviation for 'talk to you later'.
'UK' is the abbreviation for 'United Kingdom'.
'Jan' is the abbreviation for 'January'.

Practice Questions

1) **a)** rhino
   b) email (or e-mail)
   c) flu

These are the abbreviations of the longer words.

2) **a)** dinosaur
   b) television
   c) laboratory

These are the full versions of the abbreviations.

3) **a)** initialism — 'CD' = compact disc.
   b) abbreviation — 'approx' = approximately.
   c) acronym — 'NASA' = National Aeronautical Space Agency.
   d) initialism — 'DVD' = digital versatile disc.
   e) initialism — 'BBC' = British Broadcasting Corporation.

Abbreviations are shortened versions of words. Initialisms take the first letter of every word in a phrase and pronounce each letter separately. Acronyms use the first letters of words in a phrase to make a new word.

PAGES 52-53 — IRONY AND RHETORICAL QUESTIONS

1) **a)**, **c)** and **e)** no tick
   b) and **d)** tick

Situational irony is when the opposite happens to what the reader expects.

PAGES 54-55 — IDIOMS, CLICHÉS AND PROVERBS

1) **a)** You're going to end up in trouble if you carry on like this.
   b) I put a lot of effort into my maths homework.
   c) It's time to give up.
   d) I wish the politician would stop avoiding the issue.
   e) My little brother is really annoying me.

Answers may vary for these questions, but make sure you have given the literal meaning for each sentence.

PAGES 56-57 — SYNONYMS AND ANTONYMS

Warm-Up Activity

Here are some examples:
'wise' — some synonyms are: clever, intelligent, shrewd.
* — some antonyms are: naive, foolish, daft.*
'love' — some synonyms are: adore, cherish, like.
* — some antonyms are: hate, dislike, abhor.*
'brave' — some synonyms are: bold, courageous, gallant.
* — some antonyms are: cowardly, afraid, scared.*
'fast' — some synonyms are: rapid, quick, speedy.
* — some antonyms are: slow, plodding, unhurried.*

Practice Questions

1) **a)** hopeless
   b) threatening
   c) hurriedly

These are the synonyms for each of the words in bold.

2) **a)** respectful
   b) despondent
   c) stimulating

These are the antonyms for each of the words in bold.

PAGES 60-61 — READING THE TEXT

1) **a)** Eric Debuski's stage name is Lavahead.
   b) The word "frontman" (line 6) can mean the same thing as "lead vocalist".
   c) Joaquin works in a shop because in the passage it says that '"he scanned through Eric's basket", which means that he was working on a till.
   d) Eric tells Joaquin to shut his mouth because he was probably gaping at meeting a member of his favourite band.
   e) The evidence suggests that Joaquin was feeling nervous because he stutters and Eric tells him to shut his mouth, probably because he is gaping. He also feels excited, because it was "the most exciting thing that had happened".

Try to mention all of the relevant information when you're writing an answer to a comprehension question.

PAGES 66-67 — COMPREHENSION QUESTION PRACTICE

MULTIPLE CHOICE PRACTICE

1) **D** The passage says that Flashman was "wilder and more flurried than ever" (line 2).

2) **C** Scud is the same person as East. There are only three people involved in the fight: Tom, Flashman and East. At the end of the extract Diggs says, "And you have got a nasty eye, Scud" (line 25), and East replies, which suggests that "East" and "Scud" are different names for the same person.

3) **B** 'relentless' means the same as 'persistent'.

4) **E** 'Surlily' means the same as 'grumpily'.

5) **C** Tom says "He can't be very bad" after seeing Flashman walk away "so well" (line 21). This shows that he means that Flashman's injury is not very bad.

6) **D** Tom's "enemy" is Flashman, who is also referred to as "Flashey" (line 27).

STANDARD ANSWER PRACTICE

1) Various answers possible. E.g. The boys were "frightened" (line 7 and 11) and Tom was "scared out of his wits" (line 8). The characters' anxiety is also shown by the way they "sprang to their legs" (line 7) and that Tom cried out "What shall we do?" (line 14).

2) The phrase "cheap enough too" means that their injuries were worth it if it means that they have seen the last of their "old friend Flashey" (line 27).

3) The writer wants the readers to side with Tom and East because Flashman is presented as a bully. In the last line it says Flashman "never laid a finger on them again", which implies that he was a bully.

4) The writer creates a mixed mood with the last line. It is a positive ending, because it says that Flashman "never laid finger on either of them again", which means that the bully had been beaten. However, the phrase "They had done with Flashman in one sense" makes the ending tense because it suggests that Flashman got back at them in another sense.

Remember, if you are not sure about an answer, go back to the information in the text to help you guess.

PAGES 70-71 — MAKE A PLAN

1) **a)** and **b)** Various answers possible.

Make sure your plan for a) includes points for the introduction, argument and conclusion of the essay. Make sure your plan for b) has points for a gripping beginning, at least one interesting event in the middle, and an ending that brings it to a conclusion.

PAGES 72-73 — WRITE IN PARAGRAPHS

1) Following another run-in with Mr Ulrichson, Gary had awaited his verdict nervously. // "Gary, this is the third time you've been brought to my office for being late. I would have thought a 17 year old like you would know better," the headmaster said, "but I think I know the perfect punishment — Mr Levis needs some help with the junior hockey team and I remember you used to be very good at hockey, you might even enjoy it." // That was three weeks ago, and since then Gary had been coming to the threadbare pitch every week to help with the coaching. This was a task he didn't enjoy — he disliked the children and he despised standing in the cold watching them play hockey. // There was one child he truly hated: Wesley Fenton. Wesley had been a nuisance right from the start. He enjoyed tying Gary's shoelaces together when he wasn't looking and took every opportunity to hit the ball as hard as he could at Gary. // "Stupid kids!" thought Gary, as it started to rain again. "Stupid, rotten, silly kids!"

There should be a new paragraph when something changes.

PAGES 74-76 — MAKE IT INTERESTING

1) **a)** Various answers possible, e.g. 'nearby park', 'creaky swings', 'slippery slide', 'rickety roundabout'.

b) Various answers possible, e.g. 'Old Mr Brown', 'stubborn cats', 'naughty cats'.

c) Various answers possible, e.g. 'physical violence', 'terrible violence', 'bare aggression', 'loud shouting', 'awful film'.

Make sure that the adjectives you added make sense in the sentence.

2) **a)** Various answers possible, e.g. 'consumed' or 'devoured', 'starving' or 'famished', 'disgusting' or 'horrible'.

b) Various answers possible, e.g. 'dashed' or 'sprinted', 'gloomy' or 'murky', 'tripped' or 'slipped', 'bashed' or 'bruised'.

c) Various answers possible, e.g. 'delightful' or 'fantastic', 'loved' or 'enjoyed', 'hated' or 'criticised'.

If you struggled to find a different word, try looking in a thesaurus.

PAGE 77 — WRITING PRACTICE

WRITING TECHNIQUES

1) **a)** Various answers possible, e.g. 'It was a glorious day, so I ambled to the beach. First I built a massive sandcastle, then I gobbled a delicious ice cream.'

b) Various answers possible, e.g. 'The enormous ogre was hideous. I felt so terrified that I crept behind a jagged rock and skulked there until he stomped away.'

c) Various answers possible, e.g. '"Quick, give me the biggest fishing rod!" I yelled. I had seen a sudden movement in the murky depths. "Here you go," gasped Timmy, throwing me the rod. "It might not be sturdy enough — the Loch Ness monster is enormous. Here, take the reinforced net as well."'

You can add and replace adjectives, verbs and connectives to make the sentences more interesting. Try to use a variety of types and lengths of sentences to make your writing flow better.

2) **a)** Various answers possible, e.g. 'The sky was like freshly whipped cream.'

b) Various answers possible, e.g. 'The meal was as hot as the surface of the sun.'

c) Various answers possible, e.g. 'His hair was like the thatched roof of a tumbledown cottage.'

Try to make your similes appeal to the reader's senses, so they can clearly picture what you're describing.

WRITING FICTION

1) **a)** Various answers possible, e.g. 'cruel', 'sneering', 'stooped', 'twisted', 'powerful'.

b) Various answers possible, e.g. 'jolly', 'friendly', 'old', 'chubby', 'laughing'.

c) Various answers possible, e.g. 'gruff', 'hairy', 'huge', 'gentle', 'strong'.

Picture your characters as clearly as you can. Think about how they look, sound and act.

2) **a)** Various answers possible, e.g. 'A dark, crooked tower near the top of a forbidding mountain.'

b) Various answers possible, e.g. 'A cheerful, whitewashed cottage with a bright blue front door. The front garden is full of roses, and inside there is the warm smell of baking bread.'

c) Various answers possible, e.g. 'A cosy den in a bright, sun-dappled forest. The floor is soft and mossy, and the space is filled with giant, pillowy armchairs and sturdy wooden furniture.'

Add as much detail to your descriptions as you can. Try to picture exactly where your character would live.

3) **a)** and **b)** Various answers possible.

Make sure your plans include points for the beginning, middle and end of your story.

4) Various answers possible.

Remember to use the techniques you've learnt to make your writing interesting. If you decide to answer b), check you have spelt the characters' names correctly, that you have copied the same style of writing, and have continued the story so it makes sense.

WRITING NON-FICTION

1) **a) – c)** Various answers possible.

Make sure your plans include points for the introduction, argument and conclusion of your essay.

2) Various answers possible.

Make sure you use the right sort of writing style. Question a) should be informative and balanced, and should be written in an informal style. Question b) should be persuasive, and should be written in a formal style. Question c) should include lots of interesting descriptions, and should be informal.

Index